THE BOOK OF GENESIS

The Bible for School and Home

by J. Paterson Smyth

The Book of Genesis

Moses and the Exodus

Joshua and the Judges

The Prophets and Kings

When the Christ Came:
The Highlands of Galilee

When the Christ Came:
The Road to Jerusalem

St. Matthew

St. Mark

The Bible for School and Home

THE BOOK OF GENESIS

by

J. Paterson Smyth

YESTERDAY'S CLASSICS

ITHACA, NEW YORK

Cover and arrangement © 2017 Yesterday's Classics, LLC.

This edition, first published in 2017 by Yesterday's Classics, an imprint of Yesterday's Classics, LLC, is an unabridged republication of the text originally published by Sampson Low, Marston & Co., Ltd. For the complete listing of the books that are published by Yesterday's Classics, please visit www.yesterdaysclassics.com. Yesterday's Classics is the publishing arm of the Baldwin Online Children's Literature Project which presents the complete text of hundreds of classic books for children at www.mainlesson.com.

ISBN: 978-1-59915-484-8

Yesterday's Classics, LLC
PO Box 339
Ithaca, NY 14851

CONTENTS

GENERAL INTRODUCTION

I

This series of books is intended for two classes of teachers:

1. *For Teachers in Week Day and Sunday Schools.* For these each book is divided into complete lessons. The lesson will demand preparation. Where feasible there should be diligent use of commentaries and of any books indicated in the notes. *As a general rule* I think the teacher should not bring the book at all to his class if he is capable of doing without it. He should make copious notes of the subject. The lesson should be thoroughly studied and digested beforehand, with all the additional aids at his disposal, and it should come forth at the class warm and fresh from his own heart and brain. But I would lay down no rigid rule about the use of the Lesson Book. To some it may be a burden to keep the details of a long lesson in the memory; and, provided the subject has been very carefully studied, the Lesson Book, with its salient points carefully marked in coloured pencil, may be a considerable help. Let each do what seems best in his particular case, only taking care to satisfy his conscience that it is not done through

1

laziness, and that he can really do best for his class by the plan which he adopts.

2. *For Parents* who would use it in teaching their children at home. They need only small portions, brief little lessons of about ten minutes each night. For these each chapter is divided into short sections. I should advise that on the first night only the Scripture indicated should be read, with some passing remarks and questions to give a grip of the story. That is enough. Then night after night go on with the teaching, taking as much or as little as one sees fit.

I have not written out the teaching in full as a series of readings which could be read over to the child without effort or thought. With this book in hand a very little preparation and adaptation will enable one to make the lesson more interesting and more personal and to hold the child's attention by questioning. Try to get his interest. Try to make him talk. Make the lesson conversational. Don't preach.

II

HINTS FOR TEACHING

An ancient Roman orator once laid down for his pupils the three-fold aim of a teacher:

1. *Placere* (to interest).

2. *Docere* (to teach).

3. *Movere* (to move).

1. To interest the audience (in order to teach them).

2. To teach them (in order to move them).

3. To move them to action.

On these three words of his I hang a few suggestions on the teaching of this set of Lessons.

1. *Placere (to interest)*

I want especially to insist on attention to this rule. Some teachers seem to think that to interest the pupils is a minor matter. It is not a minor matter and the pupils will very soon let you know it. Believe me, it is no waste of time to spend hours during the week in planning to excite their interest to the utmost. Most of the complaints of inattention would cease at once if the teacher would give more study to rousing their interest. After all, there is little use in knowing the facts of your subject, and being anxious about the souls of the pupils, if all the time that you are teaching, these pupils are yawning and taking no interest in what you say. I know some have more aptitude for teaching than others. Yet, after considerable experience of teachers whose lesson was a weariness to the flesh, and of teachers who never lost attention for a moment, I am convinced, on the whole, that the power to interest largely depends on the previous preparation.

Therefore do not content yourself with merely studying the teaching of this series. Read widely and freely. Read not only commentaries, but books that will give local interest and colour—books that will throw valuable sidelights on your sketch.

But more than reading is necessary. You know the meaning of the expression, *"Put yourself in his place."* Practise that in every Bible story, using your imagination, living in the scene, experiencing, as far as you can, every feeling of the actors. To some this is no effort at all. They feel their cheeks flushing and their eyes growing moist as they project themselves involuntarily into the scene before them. But though it be easier to some than to others, it is in some degree possible to all, and the interest of the lesson largely depends on it. I have done my best in these books to help the teacher in this respect. But no man can help another much. Success will depend entirely on the effort to "put yourself in his place."

In reading the Bible chapter corresponding to each lesson, I suggest that the teacher should read part of the chapter, rather than let the pupils tire themselves by "reading round." My experience is that this "reading round" is a fruitful source of listlessness. When his verse is read, the pupil can let his mind wander till his turn comes again, and so he loses all interest. I have tried, with success, varying the monotony. I would let them read the first round of verses in order; then I would make them read out of the regular order, as I called their names; and sometimes, if the lesson were long, I would again and again interrupt by reading a group of verses myself, making remarks as I went on. To lose their interest is fatal.

4

I have indicated also in the lessons that you should not unnecessarily give information yourself. Try to question it *into* them. If you tell them facts which they have just read, they grow weary. If you ask a question, and then answer it yourself when they miss it, you cannot keep their attention. Send your questions around in every sort of order, or want of order. Try to puzzle them—try to surprise them. Vary the form of the question, if not answered, and always feel it to be a defeat if you ultimately fail in getting the answer you want.

2. Docere (to teach)

You interest the pupil in order that you may *teach*. Therefore teach definitely the Lesson that is set you. Do not be content with interesting him. Do not be content either with drawing spiritual teaching. Teach the facts before you. Be sure that God has inspired the narration of them for some good purpose.

When you are dealing with Old Testament characters, do not try to shirk or to condone evil in them. They were not faultless saints. They were men like ourselves, whom God was helping and bearing with, as He helps and bears with us, and the interest of the story largely depends on the pupil realizing this.

In the Old Testament books of this series you will find very full chapters written on the Creation, the Fall, the Flood, the election of Jacob, the Sun standing still, the slaughter of Canaanites, and other such subjects. In connection with these I want to say something that

5

especially concerns teachers. Your pupils, now or later, can hardly avoid coming in contact with the flippant scepticism so common nowadays, which makes jests at the story of the sun standing still, and talks of the folly of believing that all humanity was condemned because Eve ate an apple thousands of years ago. This flippant tone is "in the air." They will meet with it in their companions, in the novels of the day, in popular magazine articles on their tables at home. You have, many of you, met with it yourselves; you know how disturbing it is; and you probably know, too, that much of its influence on people arises from the narrow and unwise teaching of the Bible in their youth. Now you have no right to ignore this in your teaching of the Bible. You need not talk of Bible difficulties and their answers. You need not refer to them at all. But teach the truth that will take the sting out of these difficulties when presented in after-life.

To do this requires trouble and thought. We have learned much in the last fifty years that has thrown new light for us on the meaning of some parts of the Bible; which has, at any rate, made doubtful some of our old interpretations of it. We must not ignore this. There are certain traditional theories which some of us still insist on teaching as God's infallible truth, whereas they are really only human opinions about it, which may possibly be mistaken. As long as they are taught as human opinions, even if we are wrong, the mistake will do no harm. But if things are taught as God's infallible truth, to be believed on peril of doubting God's Word, it may do grave mischief, if in after-life the pupil find them seriously disputed, or perhaps false. A shallow, unthinking man, finding part of his teaching false, which has been associated in his mind with the most solemn sanctions of religion, is in danger of letting the whole go. Thus many of our young people drift into hazy doubt about the Bible. Then we get troubled about their beliefs, and give them books of Christian evidences to win them back by explaining that what was taught them in childhood was not *quite* correct, and needs now to be modified by a broader and slightly different view. But we go on as before with the younger generation, and expose them in their turn to the same difficulties.

Does it not strike you that, instead of this continual planning to win men back from unbelief, it might be worth while to try the other method of not exposing them to unbelief? Give them the more careful and intelligent teaching at first, and so prepare them to meet the difficulties by-and-by.

I have no wish to advocate any so-called "advanced" teaching. Much of such teaching I gravely object to. But there are truths of which there is no question amongst thoughtful people, which somehow are very seldom taught to the young, though ignorance about them in after-life leads to grave doubt and misunderstanding. Take, for example, the gradual, progressive nature of God's teaching in Scripture, which makes the Old Testament teaching as a whole lower than that of the New. This is certainly no doubtful question, and the knowledge of it is necessary for an intelligent study of

Scripture. I have dealt with it where necessary in some of the books of this series.

I think, too, our teaching on what may seem to us doubtful questions should be more fearless and candid. If there are two different views each held by able and devout men, do not teach your own as the infallibly true one, and ignore or condemn the other. For example, do not insist that the order of creation must be accurately given in the first chapter of Genesis. You may think so; but many great scholars, with as deep a reverence for the Bible as you have, think that inspired writers were circumscribed by the science of their time. Do not be too positive that the story of the Fall *must be* an exactly literal narrative of facts. If you believe that it is I suppose you must tell your pupil so. But do not be afraid to tell him also that there are good and holy and scholarly men who think of it as a great old-world allegory, like the parable of the Prodigal Son, to teach in easy popular form profound lessons about sin. Endeavor in your Bible teaching "to be thoroughly truthful: to assert nothing as certain which is not certain, nothing as probable which is not probable, and nothing as more probable than it is." Let the pupil see that there are some things that we cannot be quite sure about, and let him gather insensibly from your teaching the conviction that truth, above all things, is to be loved and sought, and that religion has never anything to fear from discovering the truth. If we could but get this healthy, manly, common-sense attitude adopted now in teaching the Bible to young people, we should, with

God's blessing, have in the new generation a stronger and more intelligent faith.

3. Movere (to move)

All your teaching is useless unless it have this object: to move the heart, to rouse the affections toward the love of God, and the will toward the effort after the blessed life. You interest in order to teach. You teach in order to move. *That* is the supreme object. Here the teacher must be left largely to his own resources. One suggestion I offer: don't preach. At any rate, don't preach much lest you lose grip of your pupils. You have their attention all right while their minds are occupied by a carefully prepared lesson; but wait till you close your Bible, and, assuming a long face, begin, "And now, boys," etc. and straightway they know what is coming, and you have lost them in a moment.

Do not change your tone at the application of your lesson. Try to keep the teaching still conversational. Try still in this more spiritual part of your teaching to question into them what you want them to learn. Appeal to the judgment and to the conscience. I can scarce give a better example than that of our Lord in teaching the parable of the Good Samaritan. He first interested His pupil by putting His lesson in an attractive form, and then He did not append to it a long, tedious moral. He simply asked the man before Him, "Which of these three *thinkest thou?*"—i.e., "What do you think about it?" The interest was still kept up. The man, pleased at the appeal to his judgment, replied promptly, "He that showed mercy on him;" and on the instant came the quick rejoinder, "Go, and do thou likewise." Thus the lesson ends. Try to work on that model.

Now, while forbidding preaching to your pupils, may I be permitted a little preaching myself? This series of lessons is intended for Sunday schools as well as week-day schools. It is of Sunday-school teachers I am thinking in what I am now about to say. I cannot escape the solemn feeling of the responsibility of every teacher for the children in his care. Some of these children have little or no religious influence exerted on them for the whole week except in this one hour with you. Do not make light of this work. Do not get to think, with good-natured optimism, that all the nice, pleasant children in your class are pretty sure to be Christ's soldiers and servants by-and-by. Alas! for the crowds of these nice, pleasant children, who, in later life, wander away from Christ into the ranks of evil. Do not take this danger lightly. Be anxious; be prayerful; be terribly in earnest, that the one hour in the week given you to use be wisely and faithfully used.

But, on the other hand, be very hopeful too, because of the love of God. He will not judge you hardly. Remember that He will bless very feeble work, if it be your best. Remember that He cares infinitely more for the children's welfare than you do, and, therefore, by His grace, much of the teaching about which you are despondent may bring forth good fruit in the days to come. Do you know the lines about "The Noisy Seven"?—

"I wonder if he remembers—
　　Our sainted teacher in heaven—
The class in the old grey schoolhouse,
　　Known as the 'Noisy Seven'?

"I wonder if he remembers
　　How restless we used to be.
Or thinks we forget the lesson
　　Of Christ and Gethsemane?

"I wish I could tell the story
　　As he used to tell it then;
I'm sure that, with Heaven's blessing,
　　It would reach the hearts of men.

"I often wish I could tell him,
　　Though we caused him so much pain
By our thoughtless, boyish frolic,
　　His lessons were not in vain.

"I'd like to tell him how Willie,
　　The merriest of us all,
From the field of Balaclava
　　Went home at the Master's call.

"I'd like to tell him how Ronald,
　　So brimming with mirth and fun,
Now tells the heathen of India
　　The tale of the Crucified One.

"I'd like to tell him how Robert,
　　And Jamie, and George, and 'Ray,'
Are honoured in the Church of God—
　　The foremost men of their day.

11

"I'd like, yes, I'd like to tell him
　　What his lesson did for me;
And how I am trying to follow
　　The Christ of Gethsemane.

"Perhaps he knows it already,
　　For Willie has told him, maybe,
That we are all coming, coming
　　Through Christ of Gethsemane.

"How many besides I know not
　　Will gather at last in heaven,
The fruit of that faithful sowing,
　　But the sheaves are already seven."

THE CREATION STORY

Lecture to the Teacher

I

I begin with a quotation from a well-known English scientist (Sir William Henry Preece, K.C.B., F.R.S., etc.):

"In all the Literature of all the languages there is no poem so magnificent as the first chapter of the Book of Genesis. It dashes off with a master's hand in a few bold words the history of a million years. The first fact chronicled is: 'In the beginning God created the Heavens and the earth,' and the next: 'God said, "Let us make man in our image after our likeness."' We are not enlightened, as to the tools or processes by which these things were fashioned, or to the period occupied in the operations. Creation may and probably is going on still, for new wonders are being discovered every day, and there is no sign of finality. Our range of observation is a mere dot in the vast expanse of space.

"It was the fashion in the days of my youth to regard Science and Religion as antagonistic. It is so no longer. I have known more religious men in the ranks of Science than in the Army of the Church. My two great Masters in Electricity were Faraday and Kelvin. They were eminently true religious men. The Facts of Science, when properly interpreted, invariably support the truths of Religion."

Where did this wonderful Creation Story originate? We do not know. How old is it? We do not know. We know only that in its substance it is ages older than the Book of Genesis where it finds its present place.

A most interesting fact brought out by thoughtful Bible study is that the Bible was not formed all at once but grew gradually. Long before our present Old Testament books God was helping men by earlier fragmentary teaching, oral teaching, folklore told in tribal gatherings and around the ancient camp fires; written teaching perhaps reaching back before Abraham, when writing was quite common in the early world. We can tell very little about it but we have clear traces of its existence. Just as we know of the existence of long lost primeval life-forms through fossils embedded in the rocks, so we know of the existence of this long lost ancient literature through its traces embedded in the Bible.

The Old Testament writers, you will remember, keep repeatedly telling us of the old lost documents existing long before themselves. They tell us that they are quoting from, e.g., the Book of the Wars of the Lord (Numbers xxi. 4), the Book of Jasher (2 Samuel i. 18), Books of Gad and Nathan (1 Chronicles xxix. 29, and

2 Chronicles xii. 15); the Books of Shemaiah and Iddo (2 Chronicles vii. 15); the Book of Jehu (2 Chronicles xx. 34); etc., etc.

I want, in passing, to emphasize for you the fact stated by the inspired writers themselves that they wrote their histories of past ages much in the way that Mr. Green or Professor Gardiner or any other historian wrote his history. This is most important to remember in the scare about Higher Criticism which some of you know about. You would never think of doubting these historians' account of William the Conqueror merely because they wrote their histories 900 years after his death. Of course you would believe that they studied the books of earlier historians and old letters and parchments and inscriptions and monuments. And if all the libraries and museums which contained these should be burned down to-morrow you would surely think it unreasonable if people should say that we have no good grounds for believing that William the Conqueror ever lived.

Yet something of this kind is what makes people uneasy in the statements of what is called "Higher Criticism." Scholars express the opinion that the Pentateuch *in its present completed form* was written centuries later than Moses' day. Then somebody suggests that if that be so it cannot be trustworthy history, in fact that the writer must have been romancing a good deal. It is a steadying thought to keep in mind that the writers keep telling us that their histories were so much made up out of pre-existing documents. On reading Green's "History of the English People" you know that

300 years before him there were several less complete printed histories—and 300 years earlier still there were still less complete manuscript chronicles, and 300 years farther back there were separate uncollected annals, and state papers and letters and documents of various kinds. Thus gradually by successive editing English history grew. And thus also gradually Bible history grew, under the care of that inspired Church whose history it was.

No one can tell from what age of the world our Hebrew Creation Stories came into the Bible. We have two of them thus lifted in side by side in Genesis. One of them in the first chapter, the other in the second. They differ in the titles "God" and "Lord God" given to the Creator; they differ, too, in details, but they agree in the grand claim that in the beginning GOD (not a great crocodile, nor an elephant, nor a set of fighting deities), but GOD created the heavens and the earth.

What strange fancies this Creation Story sets stirring! How far back does it go? Did you ever wonder what the ancient world did for want of a Bible before the Bible was written? How did men during all these centuries learn anything about God? Had they this Creation Story in substance handed down perhaps by word of mouth in the folklore of the early Hebrew race? Was it the first inspired Bible of the primitive world? Did Moses's mother teach it to her boy as she nursed him in the palace? Was it part of the religious knowledge which made Joseph such a hero? Did Abram receive it in Ur of the Chaldees? Had God already guided inspired men to teach the infant world The Creation, The Fall, The

Story of the Flood, as a sort of "Bible before the Bible" for those ancient days?

We cannot answer these questions. We find the story standing in the Book of Genesis. And we know that it came from far earlier sources. That is all we know.

II

Now, we are to consider this old Creation Story.

I don't think any thoughtful reader can study it without being impressed with two things: its simplicity and its grandeur.

Its simplicity lies on the very surface. It evidently belongs in its simple form to simple people in the simple child ages of the old world. There are no scientific statements. There are no learned descriptions. Just the simple story for simple people in the simple child ages.

Its simplicity, I say, lies on the surface. But fully to realize its grandeur and sublimity you must compare this Hebrew Creation Story with some of the Creation Stories of other races.

Some fifty years ago a sensation was created in the religious world by the discovery of a similar Creation Story and Deluge Story in Abraham's old home in Chaldea. It is written on clay tablets, and in its origin goes back probably to Abraham's day. It was studied with deep interest both because it came from Abraham's country and because it resembled our Genesis account.

Both the Chaldean account and the Bible account agree in having the simplicity of an old world story for the child races of the world. But if you want to feel in full force the meaning of inspiration, you have only to compare the two stories, to compare the gross polytheism and superstition into which the poor stupid age naturally drifted—and the pure, dignified, sublime account given to teach a chosen race who should bear the torch of God's light for humanity.

Reading the two together you feel at once how like they are and yet how unlike. You see that they are both simple stories in simple form for the child races of the world.

But one tells in simple childlike way of many gods with evil human passions at the head of creation. The other tells in the same simple childlike way of one God, holy and just and good who created everything in the heavens and the earth, who made the sun and the moon which the Chaldeans worshipped, and the great bulls to which the Egyptians prayed, and who as the crown and summit of His whole creation "made MAN in His image, after His likeness, and gave him dominion over the fish and the sea, and over the fowl of the air, and over the cattle, and over all the earth." Some think that the Chaldean story is a corruption of a purer original. Others think that God's inspiration enabled the Chosen Race to purify an older story and to see with the keen intuition derived from on high, that "In the beginning GOD created the heavens and the earth."

But, however this may have been, no one can compare this Hebrew statement with the Chaldean or Egyptian or any other in the world without a sense of the presence of God.

A deep sense of God's inspiration in the Old Testament comes from comparing it with the writings and thoughts of other nations around. When you read of the dark ages of Greece and Rome, the stories of their filthy gods and goddesses, and the deeds of their brave, cruel, boastful men—it never occurs to you to expect any trace of sorrow for sin or longing after holiness. Then turn to read the early prophets of Israel pleading only for righteousness and the psalmists crying and longing after God and mourning in deep agony for their sins, and you feel at once this sense of God's presence, of God's inspiration, of God's great purpose to raise up one nation as the teachers and prophets of the world.

In deepest sincerity I am saying what I feel. No man can honestly place the writings of Scripture beside any other writings of their time without confessing that the best proof of the inspiration of the Bible is the Bible itself. Has any man ever found conviction of sin and conversion to God resulting from the study of Greek or Roman classics? We find it continually resulting from the study of the Hebrew classics. We believe that the Bible is inspired because it inspires.

III

Many difficulties that have been found by superficial readers in the story of creation arise from misunderstandings which should have been corrected in us in our childhood and which it is our business to correct in the pupils of our day. I don't mean that we should necessarily speak to them of doubts and difficulties; but that we should avoid the teaching and correct the misapprehensions which lead to such doubts and difficulties.

Take, for instance, the vague impression in many minds that science demands a much greater antiquity for the world than the Bible accounts would allow. This impression has been, I think, originated mainly by the statement in the margin of many old Bibles that Creation took place B.C. 4004. Of course, this marginal note is no part of the Bible. It is but a mere human conjecture inserted 300 years ago. But it has turned out to be a mischievous conjecture. Because it is on a page of the Bible, people have unconsciously accepted it as of some authority, and feel troubled when they read in authoritative scientific works that probably four million and four[1] would be nearer to the truth. Tell the pupils

[1] The 4 has an amusing appearance of exactness, as if there were really some good grounds for fixing a date. In this age it is a surprising and interesting study, that of the efforts made by the greatest minds in the Church for centuries to settle this question. The great majority, from Eusebius to Archbishop Ussher, agreed that the date must be B.C. 4004. They were not content even with fixing the year. In the seventeenth century Dr. John Lightfoot, Vice-Chancellor of the University of

to draw a pencil mark through that 4004; and in future when you read of the millions of years that go to make a limestone rock, and the millions or billions that may go to make a planet—when your mind almost reels at the stupendousness of the thought, remember that the Bible puts no difficulty in your path by setting limits to the time. This marvellous old Creation story simply says *"In the beginning,"* which may have been thousands, or millions, or billions of years ago. In the Beginning God created the heavens and the earth.

So far for statements that are clearly *not* in the Bible. Next comes a statement that *is* in the Bible: that Creation was finished in six days. I suppose nobody now believes, except the children, that the Creation was finished in six literal days of twenty-four hours each. The children believe it still; and one sometimes feels it a pity that we have to correct them. For this story, belonging to the child races of the primitive world, has been apparently with intention cast in this simple form, so that it should be intelligible to even the simplest minds in all the ages. Perhaps the earliest writer or teacher of it thought—no doubt, the primitive races who learned it thought—that the Creation was begun on the first morning of a certain week, and cleanly finished on the last night, as a carpenter might finish off his week's work. It was a simple notion, but sufficient for them, and nothing would have been gained by explaining to

---

Cambridge, one of the most eminent Hebraists of his time, declared, as the result of his careful calculations, that Creation took place and man was created by the Trinity on October 23rd, 4004 B.C., at nine o'clock in the morning!

them that this framework of six days might represent millions of years. It would have been premature. It would have been bewildering to men who could form no clear conception of large numbers or long periods of time.[1] It would have been utterly useless for the purpose intended of helping men's lives nearer to God. People were but big children, needing children's teaching for their simple, undeveloped minds. The teaching must be true, but popular and elementary. Does anyone seriously believe that it would have been well to teach them in an accurate science lesson about the "HOW" of Creation; to teach them, perhaps, about evolution, and the nebular theory, and the "uncompounded homogeneous, gaseous condition of matter," and the vast stretches of time needed for making the universe? Of what use would all this bewildering knowledge have been in teaching the one fact of supreme import for them to save them from grovelling, debasing polytheism; that it was God, holy and good, who made all things; and that the crown and summit of His work was man?

I don't think it matters at all that the early simple minds should have so read the Creation story, or that simple people should still believe that the world was created in six literal days. Good Christians and holy men in all ages have done so, and their religion was none the worse for it. But it matters very much if people insist that this is the only possible belief consistent with Scripture, that the truth of inspiration is pledged to

[1]Mr. Gladstone emphasizes this point in his *Impregnable Rock of Holy Scripture;* and points to his studies in Homer for proof that the early men could not clearly comprehend large numbers.

this belief, and that to doubt it is to doubt the inspired Word of God.

For the framework of six scenes or days is no essential part of the story. And the writer of this Book of Genesis seems to go out of his way to show this. For, as I have said, he gives you a second Creation story side by side with the first (*ch.* ii. 4-26), differing from it as one of the Gospels differs from another, yet helping to make the lesson more complete. This second version is not at all arranged in the six days' framework; nay, it rather thinks of Creation as done in one day—*"in the day"* (ii. 4)—which caused a great deal of controversy for ages in the Church. This second version also is not particular to give the same order of Creation; while the teaching about God and man is just the same in them both. The Creation Psalm, also (civ.), which is a paraphrase of this story, lays no stress on the time or on the order of the Creation. And the same is true of all the passages in the Bible praising God for His creative work. Surely this should make it at least probable that to teach the time and the exact order was no part of the object of inspiration, but to teach the great lesson, so essential to religion, that all things come of God.

IV

But let there be no mistake here. Let there be no flippant talk that because the purpose of the Bible is religious and moral, therefore the account of the Creation here is to be treated lightly, or as unworthy the attention of scientific men. For this Creation story is at the foundation of all science as well as of all religion. Even men who doubt its supernatural origin must at least see what it has done for the world in saving it from subjection to the grotesque myths and nature-worship and polytheism which grew wild in the world, and which would have made a true science of nature impossible. Where the sun and moon were gods, and the crocodile and ox were reverenced as divine, and men bowed down in fear at the many deities warring in the stormy heavens, a true science of nature could not be. Where the powers of nature were worshipped and feared, there could never be the confidence or freedom needed for the study of nature. To the Hebrew poets and prophets alone there is calm and peace. They have learned the inspired Creation Story. To them there is no power in nature save the one supreme will—snow and hail, fire and vapour, stormy wind, fulfilling His word. All through the Bible runs that deep and reverent teaching of which the keynote is struck in these opening words of Genesis, and whose influence has given to mankind the liberty which made possible the scientific attitude of mind.

But, people say, it is not a scientifically correct account of Creation, and, therefore, could not be inspired by God. Perhaps it is not a scientifically correct account; but does it follow, therefore, that it is not inspired of God? When a child asks us questions about the phenomena of nature, do we give him scientifically correct accounts? Would it be wise to do so? Would he understand us? We consider the capacity of the child's mind, and impart to him *as much truth as he is capable of receiving* on the matter in a simple, imperfect, popular way. We aim at a teaching that will be intelligible, that will not teach him what is false, and that will not have to be unlearned by him by-and-by, when his mind grows able to understand the full scientifically accurate account. And if some scientific professor should object that our explanation was very imperfect, we should think that though that professor might know a good deal about science, he knew very little about teaching children.

I want you to see that it is an entirely false issue when you ask: "Is this a completely scientific account of Creation?" The question is rather: "Does this Genesis story accomplish what seems to be its purpose?"

Is it not simple enough for the youngest child in our Sunday schools to understand it, and remember it?

Is it not lofty and elevating enough for the philosopher in its conceptions of the greatness of God and the dignity of man as the child of God?

Is it not helpful to science in its delivering men from the terror of nature; in its conception of the unity and universality of creation; in its introducing the great idea of creating—i.e., making out of nothing—which pagan nations unaided have always been unable to attain?

And does it not fulfil the further condition that the *simple old child-lesson will never have to be laid aside,* but only enlarged, and its details filled in? For all the ages up to this it has served its purpose; but men say now that it does so no longer. Science has been teaching us the marvellous discoveries of evolution—of germs of life developed through ever higher stages for myriads of years; and foolish, hasty people say, "The Bible is now disproved. All things have come not by direct creation of God, but by slow, age-long development from lower stages." Perhaps this theory will be superseded by a better; but at present it seems a very probable theory. Does it overthrow the Bible? Is the old creation story contradicted if this theory be correct?

Nay, rather, has it not for thoughtful readers of the Bible received a new light and glory? Men have gone back to the old Creation story to read it again in the light of this new discovery about evolution. Many students of Scripture at first were perplexed. Then they went back. They saw at once that creation would be just as Divine and miraculous if it were slow and gradual. Doubtless God could instantaneously make a mighty oak; but surely it is no less wonderful if He should only make the little acorn, of which I could carry a dozen in my hand, and yet, every one of which contains within it a mighty oak endued with power to carry on a succession of mighty oaks through ages to come. This roughly illustrates the difference between the idea of direct creation of a world completely fitted up at once, and that of a slow, gradual evolution which men of science at present think to be the truer theory of creation.

Men saw, I repeat, that the Creation story was at least not incompatible with evolution. Then they examined the old document more closely in the light of this new science, and they saw that there was absolutely no warrant in it for looking on the world as a ready-made piece of work. They saw in the inspired story—what men had not looked for before—a foreshadowing of this magnificent process. It reveals a law of continuous development in creation. "These are the generations of the heavens when they were created." "The inspired historian saw no Almighty Hand building up the galleries of Creation; he heard no sound of hammer nor confused noise of workmen; the Spirit of the Lord moved upon the face of the deep; chaos took form and comeliness before His inspired vision; and the solar system grew through a succession of days to its present order and beauty;" and at last, when all things were ready—after how many myriads of years we know not—man came forth of the dust, the summit of the whole creation, for "God breathed into his nostrils the breath of life, and man became a living soul."

Instead, therefore, of assuming an apologetic tone for this Creation story, try to understand its purpose and its effect on life; try to realize what a check it has been on the wild growth of mythologies and debasing nature-worship; what a foundation it has made for the science and religion of the world; how it has taught, what could never have been otherwise learned, that all things come into existence through the originating will of God; that the summit of the whole Creation is man, the child of God, into whom the Divine breath has been breathed, to make him akin to the Almighty.

Learn thus a deep reverence for the story, which shall show through your teaching, and shall help your pupils of this new generation to more solemn thoughts about the Bible.

LESSON ON THE CREATION STORY

Genesis I. and II. to v. 4

Read carefully the introductory Lecture to this Lesson. Note that the teaching to be emphasized is (1) that all things come from the hand of God; (2) the dignity of man made in God's likeness, the end and summit of Creation.

§ 1. *The Creation Story*

I want you to look back a long time—to the time when you were not here in the world. How long ago? Ten, fifteen years? Was anybody here then—father? mother? Were there animals? trees? rivers? etc. All without you! How could they have got on without you! Now we go back still farther, before father, mother, or anyone that you know; go by steps or stages back to St. Paul; back to Isaiah, to Moses, to Abraham, to Noah. Back behind all; before men, women, trees, anything existed; all a mass of dull cloud and vapour, and darkness, and confusion. What does the Bible say? (*ch.* i., *v.* 2). We don't know how many thousands or millions of years ago. Was anybody here then? God. Was there ever a time when God was not in the world? What was God going to do with all that confused, cloudy mass, without form and void? To make a world. How did He begin? (*v.* 2). And then? (*v.* 3). You see how easy for God to make everything; just a brooding of His Spirit—just a word of His power. "He spake and it was done."

Now, do you know that this Creation story is probably older by far than Moses—older by far than the Book of Genesis, where it has been inserted? Perhaps in substance older than Abraham, or perhaps revealed to Abraham, and used by his children and descendants long before Moses's day as a little Bible fragment to keep their thoughts right with God.

Fancy Moses, and Joseph, and Isaac being taught this old story by their mothers in some such form as we have it to-day.

See how simply that story was taught. In seven periods, seven divisions or little chapters, or seven "days." This made it easy to remember, and to teach to the children and the simple big people in the wandering tribes. We do not think that God made everything in six exact days of twenty-four hours each; but that was the simple Eastern way of learning it.

Some people think that the whole story was perhaps revealed to the inspired writer in a vision of six scenes or days, as if a magic lantern should show it in six pictures. We do not know. Could God have made everything in six days or six hours? Yes; just as easily as in six thousand years. But the world has the appearance of having been very slowly made, and certainly took many thousands of years.

And so you have to learn to-day the story that was taught to the children, and men, and women in the early ages of the world. What does it say was made on first day (or period)? second? third? etc. What did God say of each day's work? (Question carefully but rapidly through the chapter up to *v.* 25, trying to leave on the mind the impression of the gradual, orderly way in which Creation progressed from the formless void of *v.* 2, through all the stages, until at last the earth stood ready for its final purpose; and then, when all was prepared, after perhaps enormous periods of time, God made man. *(Be careful to lead up to man's creation as the climax.)* If teachers teach it wisely, this story, so simply learned by the child-races of the world, will never have to be superseded as science advances. By-and-by, if the pupils should learn all that science may have then to tell about *how* the Creation was accomplished, the old story of their childhood, in its simple grandeur, will still remain as the eternal framework, Science only has to fill in the details.)

§ 2. The Use of the Creation Story

Now, why do you think this Creation story was so very important for men to know? Why should they care? Because they could not help caring. The cows, and horses, and lions did not want to know how they came here; but men can't help wondering and asking, Where did I come from? What am I here for? Where am I going to? Did anyone make me and all things about me? or did we just come of ourselves, by chance, with no one to care for us. If somebody made us, what sort of being was it—good or bad, loving or hostile—a god or a brute? Men could never have the courage to struggle on without knowing, or at least guessing, something of these things. Do you think they could ever find out by themselves? Who must teach them? God.

Would it make any matter if people never learned the answer to their questions? If they thought they came by chance, or that the sun and moon, or a number of not very good gods, had made them, or that some great big elephant made them, or a crocodile, as some of them thought in Egypt where Moses lived—would it matter? Why? Because if I thought that I came by chance, or was made by bad gods, or by a brutal crocodile or elephant, I should be always frightened and troubled, and I should feel that I was a low, degraded thing; so I should never be likely to rise up to a life of beautiful deeds and noble thoughts. But if I somehow found out that a noble, righteous, loving God had made me, with His own nature in me, and was watching over me as His own child, and wanted me to be noble and righteous and loving, just like Himself, would not that make a difference? Therefore God began His Bible with this glorious statement—"In the beginning God created," etc.

Would it be any comfort to the poor world of olden days? Think of the poor, simple, frightened people who did not know. They saw earthquakes, and lightning, and fierce, raging seas. They heard the wild storm-wind breaking down the trees, and the beasts of prey roaring in the forest, and they trembled, and feared, and prayed to these animals, and these strong forces of nature around them. And perhaps they asked in their wonder, Did anyone make these? Does anyone rule them? Did anyone make us? Where did we come from? Does anyone take thought for us? Can anyone help us? Can the sun and moon save us when we, in Chaldea, pray to them? Can the crocodiles and river be appeased when we sacrifice to them in Egypt? And God's answer came at last. Like a cool, soft hand upon the world's hot brow, there came this peace of God through the Creation story: "In the beginning GOD created the heaven and the earth. And GOD made two great lights, the sun and moon that ye worship; and GOD made the great monsters that you are so terribly afraid of; and GOD made you, and breathed His breath into you to make you holy. You are the greatest thing in God's creation, for you are most like to God." Would not that be a comfort to them, and a help to make them brave and good?

§ 3. Man in God's Image

Read from *v.* 26. Now we come to the final act of Creation. On what day? Yes. That is the last of the great periods of Creation. All the dead things—earth, and sun, and moon—were made. The earth was made, the animals were made; and all were good. All obeyed the law of their nature as God designed; they *had* to do it. The sun and moon could not help rising and setting, could they? But at last God was going to make the noblest thing of all—a being with some of His own divine nature in him; a being with a free will, who could obey or disobey as he pleased. So He said, "Let us make man;" and He made man. And, like a boy awaking in the morning, and wondering, and asking, "Where am I?" the man awoke into life, and rose upright, and knew at once that he was not like the beasts around him. Why? i. *v.* 26; ii. 7. "In God's image, after God's likeness." Even to us, in spite of the Fall, much of this likeness remains. There is a spark of God's nature in every one of us; we have a consciousness of God; we have a feeling within of a great eternal rule of right stamped on our soul; and when we do right or wrong, something inside us praises or blames us; and when we want to do a bad thing, it insists "you ought not;" we can't prevent it doing so; and sometimes it frightens us, and points us in the dark midnight to a great judgment hereafter. Did you ever feel this curious feeling? What do we call it? Conscience! Yes, it is the part of us where the Holy Spirit dwells, and by which He prompts us to every good thought and deed. Is this true of the beasts? (Make the children realize this difference between man and beast, and thus understand the meaning of "God's image and likeness.")

Is it not a glorious thought that man is the chief work—the crown of all God's Creation? That when Christ came to earth, it was not as an angel, but a man. Whenever you think your life insignificant, and that it does not matter whether an insignificant thing such as you does right or wrong, think that we are *related* to God—in kinship with God, as none of the beasts are. Remember this, that you are made in God's image and likeness; that we are so important in His sight that He thought it worth while spending thousands and thousands of years in preparing this earth for us as a sort of platform on which we should live, and form our characters, and grow Godlike and fit for heaven; that He thought it worth while at last, when all else failed, to come down to earth, and take our nature, and die for us. Is it not a shame to disappoint Him?

QUESTIONS FOR LESSON I

Does Bible tell how long ago God began creating the world?

What does it say?

Must six days mean six literal days?

What was created on first day?

Tell of some of the other days.

What was the final act of creation?

What does this teach us about Man? For whose sake was the world created?

THE STORY OF THE FALL

Genesis II. 15 to end, and III.

Lecture to the Teacher

I

In last lesson we learnt the Creation story, as the old child-races of the world received it many thousands of years ago, with its two great lessons:—

(1) God created the heaven and the earth.

(2) Man was the crown and blossom of all His creation.

Man was akin to God, with God's nature in him. He thus stands apart from all the rest of Creation. "God breathed into his nostrils the breath of life and man became a living soul."

At the same time, we should be mistaken in thinking that man was absolutely Godlike on account of his being made "in God's image, after His likeness." If he were, he could not have fallen. The meaning is plain. God

35

had just made the brute creatures, who were *not* "in His image." Now comes a great step upward—a being with personality, consciousness, freedom of will, and, therefore, direct moral responsibility. And thus man was like his Maker "in His image, after His likeness."

But innocence is not the highest stage of goodness. INNOCENCE is a lower thing than RIGHTEOUSNESS. And God will not be content without righteousness, which means *innocence maintained in the presence of temptation.* INNOCENCE belongs to the untried baby who has never known evil. RIGHTEOUSNESS belongs to the developed saint, who knows evil, and has been tempted by evil, but by the grace of God has resisted it.

God desired RIGHTEOUSNESS for His creatures. But for this there must first come to them the "knowledge of good and evil"—the knowledge of it even as God knows it. For God surely knows evil; as a something hateful and revolting; as a thing outside of Him altogether. And man must also know it thus, else he can never make a deliberate choice of good; never rise into the glory of moral manhood. Unless one knows both good and evil, and deliberately chooses the good, it is clear that there can be no real character.

Make no mistake here. Men sometimes say "a man must know life," "must sow his wild oats," etc., which means that he must know evil by *partaking* of it. God forbid! "Ye shall not eat of it, neither shall ye touch it, lest ye die." For all growth of character it is necessary to have to keep choosing between good and evil, and, therefore, to know evil; but the evil must be known as God knows it—as a thing *external* and to be detested.

It is most important to keep in mind this distinction between Innocence and Righteousness. Earnest, godly people often talk sentimentally about the innocence of childhood; of their regret for it, as compared with their present state of temptation and struggle. We find the sentiment frequent in poetry. You remember Hood:—

> "I remember, I remember
>   The fir-trees dark and high,
> I used to think their slender tops
>   Were close against the sky.
> It was a childish ignorance,
>   But now 'tis little joy
> To know I'm farther off from heaven
>   Than when I was a boy."

Perhaps he was, but perhaps he was not. At any rate, character can only be formed by means of temptation. That is God's will for man, and there is no use in trying to avoid it. You know how a mother would like to keep her boy always in her sight, that no evil should ever be seen or heard by him. She is afraid of school life; afraid of business life. She wants to keep her darling in the innocent stage always. It is very pathetic, but she must learn that her child, too, must come to the knowledge of good and evil, though she will pray that he may come to it by conquering the wrong. He must know good and evil. He must choose. This is God's will. All she can do is to spend her soul in prayer and effort that her boy may be nobly trained against the days of temptation.

Now we return to our story. The ancient writer or teacher has to deal with the fact patent, alas! to us as to him that the beings made by God for a high destiny are sinning and rebelling against God. So he writes his story. The parents of our race are pictured before us in the lovely world that God has made for them. They have got a fair and beautiful start in life, more so than any of us who are already tainted. They have good dispositions, good desires, no knowledge of evil, or temptation to it. They are like happy children in the presence of the great Father. But their testing-time must come. God is too desirous of good for them to spare them that. And so immediately following the story of their creation comes the story of their testing, and, alas! their fall. Look at the picture. Adam and Eve are in a beautiful garden. In the midst of it is a tree with a mystical name—the Tree of Life, and, more prominent still, for the purpose of the story, another mystical tree—the Tree of the Knowledge of Good and Evil; and lurking near this tree a serpent which speaks to them words of temptation to sin and doubt about God. Nobody can read that story without feeling there is something meant more than the mere literal story. The talking serpent and the trees with their mystical names suggest at once that, though it is a narration of facts of vital importance to each of us, yet that these facts are presented to us under an allegorical shape so prevalent in Eastern teaching. What is meant by the serpent? We get no hint in the story that it is anything but an ordinary serpent; but the Book of Revelation tells of "that old serpent the devil." It tells us also of a Tree of Life, which means eternal life and eternal communion with God. "Blessed are they who do His commandments, that they may have a right to the Tree of Life."

And what is the meaning of the other tree? What we have already said will suggest it at once. In some way—perhaps by forbidding them to eat of a literal tree; perhaps in some other way—the alternative of right and wrong is presented to the minds of Adam and Eve, and they are forced to make a choice of good or evil. In the presence of this alternative, the old childlike innocence is no longer possible. They must rise into conscious right-doing, or fall into conscious wrong. They never again now can be just as they were. A new consciousness has come into their lives, the discernment of good and evil.

Now you will probably see less difficulty in the question why God did not save them from this temptation of the serpent. No human life can grow into righteousness without temptation. From the childlike innocence in which man was created he must pass into the higher condition of moral manhood. He must no longer merely do good instinctively. He must rise into the doing of good in the presence of evil; keeping his innocence unstained in the face of temptation. Alas! that this rise should be only possible at the risk of falling! But that seems the great law of the spiritual life. Gains are always won at the risk of corresponding losses; victories at the risk of corresponding defeats. Every temptation that comes to us is an illustration. It is an opportunity of gain at the risk of a loss; an opportunity of victory at the risk of defeat.

Alas! that our first parents chose the wrong! By that "disobedience sin entered into the world, and death by sin." Shame and sorrow came into their lives; and conscience, latent, perhaps before, sprang into conscious existence in their wretched self-condemnation, as it might otherwise have sprung into existence in their glad self-approval.

It is some comfort that the enticement by itself was not sufficient to tempt them. The great evil being, who has been the curse of our race since, was at their side. No man when he is tempted must excuse himself by putting the blame of his sin on Satan; yet it is some comfort to think that all the evil thoughts and suggestions that come to us are not entirely from within. We might well despair of ourselves then. Satan, the great fallen angel, is ever watching. The test of the knowledge of good and evil had, it would seem, in long past ages come to the angels too. Some of them resisted; some of them fell (Jude, *v.* 6). And the first and chief of those who fell was Satan. Evil seems to have begun with him by his choosing to try the evil; and then he seems to have gone on from bad to worse until he came to the fearful crime of the seduction of man. Did this seal his fate beyond recovery? Is that the meaning of the terrible curse: "Because thou hast done this thing, . . . on thy belly shalt thou go, and dust shalt thou eat all the days of thy life"? Never again shalt thou rise erect in thine ancient dignity to look into the face of God. Thou shalt be for ever a degraded, crawling thing, down in the dust of the earth.

However that may be, our concern is with our own

race, and our own selves, on whom the curse of Adam's sin has fallen. How does it affect us? Does the doctrine of Original Sin mean that we are to be punished for what Adam and Eve did many thousands of years ago? Surely not. Original Sin is "the fault and corruption of the nature of every man that naturally is engendered of the offspring of Adam." We know how a child inherits the good or bad qualities of its parents or ancestors. We are most anxious to warn young people to keep life pure and noble, in view of the future days of fatherhood and motherhood, since the character of little children will be influenced by theirs. Thus it was. The first sin was the beginning of many sins. Early mankind became sinful; therefore it was easier for their children to become so, and then for theirs again. The infection spread like a plague. It was not that God devised a legal figment to condemn us; nay, but that He devised a way of deliverance from what was no figment, but an awful dread reality which clings to us all.

After the sin came the shame—the consciousness that they were naked, stripped of the innocence that made them walk unabashed before God and each other. Do not we all know when we have fallen into sin how marvellously true is that old inspired picture of the shame, and the hiding, and the fruitless effort to cover the shame with a few fig-leaves? Do we all understand equally the loving mercy of God, who did not want His poor, shamed, hiding creatures to be shamed and hiding for ever, and so has Himself provided a covering for them?

Try to learn carefully this Lesson about the Fall.

Try to make it very *real,* and of concern to each pupil. The idea has been much obscured by religious cant and unreal phrases. Teach to the children what you think they will understand of it, and last, but by no means least, when you hear the silly, flippant, sceptical talk about Eve eating an apple, and God unfairly condemning the whole world for it, do your utmost to discourage it, by explaining the Church's meaning of original sin, and by showing the wonder, and beauty, and solemnity of this story of the Fall of Man.

LESSON ON THE FALL

Read Genesis III.

This is the most important Lesson in Genesis. Prepare well for it. Let the whole be carefully planned. You cannot afford to lose any time, nor to lose the interest for a moment. I have written a very full Lesson, so that you can pick out what suits the age of your class, and leave the rest. Be very careful to make the Lesson solemn and real, and let the pupils feel that it is no mere old-world story, but that it has a close interest for them. Each one is suffering from the evil brought thus into this beautiful world many thousands of years ago. Read Milton's *Paradise Lost,* and Bunyan's *Holy War.*

COMMENTARY

V. 5. "As gods," R.V., "as God" (Elohim).

V. 8. *They heard the voice of Jehovah.* This very

ancient history of Creation and Fall is full of such expressions—i. 26, 31; ii. 2, 8, 19, etc. All this corresponds well with the simple, childlike character of the early portions of Genesis. The Great Father, through His inspired Word, is teaching His children in infancy of the race in simple lessons.—*Speaker's Commentary.*

V. 15. *The seed of the woman.* The promise is not only (1) general, i.e., that Satan and his servants shall always fight with Eve's descendants, that ultimately mankind shall, by God's help, conquer (even that is a glorious hope for the race); but also (2) particular and personal—a personal contest and a personal victory of that one Seed of the woman, who had no earthly father, and who "was manifested that He might destroy the works of the devil."

§ 1. The Siege of Mansoul

I want to tell you an old story that I read long ago. It is about a war—the Holy War it is called—and in this war is the siege of the city of MANSOUL. The great king of the country had built this city for his own use. He committed the guarding of it to the inhabitants. And he had so cleverly built the walls that they could never be broken down without the consent of those within.

The city had five entrance-gates—Ear-gate, Eye-gate, Mouth-gate, Nose-gate, Feel-gate; and they, too, were so cleverly made, that, like the walls, they could never be forced open without the consent of those inside. I have not time to tell you about the defenders. Amongst them were the brave Captain Resistance and the wise

43

old Judge Conscience, who was so well read in the laws of the king, and so brave and faithful to speak them forth at all times. I have only time to tell you the story of the trick by which the black giant Diabolus got into the town. He called a council of war, and when his generals wanted to smash down the walls and gates, "Oh, no," said he, "you cannot do that, for Mansoul is so strongly built that no one can conquer it but by its own consent. If you attack it openly, they will send to the king for help, and it is all up with us." "What shall we do, then?" they asked. "I will tell you," said he. "Let us hide our intentions with flatteries and lies; let us pretend things that will never be; let us promise that which they shall never find; and soon we shall coax them to open the gates."

So they came down next morning with friendly words, and coaxed, and promised, and lied to the soldiers. And the gates that could never have been forced from outside were opened to them by the deluded guards. The enemy rushed in and took possession of the town, and MANSOUL fell into abject slavery. The king was terribly vexed and disappointed; and the guards were utterly disgraced and shamed when the king demanded why his town had been taken.

Do you think that story has any hidden meaning? Explain: Man's Soul, Conscience, Resistance, Diabolus (Devil). Eye-gate, Ear-gate, etc. What is meant by the statement that the walls and gates could only be opened from inside? What is meant by Diabolus deceiving the garrison? Who is meant by the king? What do we call that sort of story? A parable or allegory. It is one of our

Lord's favourite ways of teaching truth. Name a few of His parables.

§ 2. *The Story of the Fall*

Now, long, long ages ago, in the very early days of the world, God inspired men to teach the world this simple, wonderful story of Adam and Eve in the Garden of Delight, and the serpent talking, and the two trees with the strange names. What names? First tell me the story. (*Get the story told rapidly and spiritedly by the children in rotation, or else question rapidly through the chapter. Have your questions prepared beforehand. Do not exceed ten minutes. Do not let the interest flag.*)

Divide into sections for examining:—

(1) *Vv.* 1-7. *Temptation and Fall.* Serpent suggesting doubt of God? Eve's defence of God? Serpent contradicts God? Accuses God of evil motive? His temptation to Eve? Pleasantness of sin in prospect? Result of the sin?

(2) *Vv.* 7-14. *Shame and hiding.* Effect of sin, shame and hiding, as contrasted with pleasantness beforehand. So with sin always. God's stern rebuke? The cowardly excuses? Adam's implied charge against God? (*v.* 12).

(3) *Vv.* 14-24. *Sentence on Adam? On Eve? Serpent?* —Specially emphasize *v.* 15, promise of Messiah. Expulsion from Eden.

Is there anything in this story like the siege of MANSOUL? What was the MANSOUL here being attacked? By whom? Could the serpent have conquered without their consent? How did he conquer at last? (*v.* 13). Whose fault, then, was it that this wrong thing was done? Was it the serpent's fault? Was he punished? How? But Adam and Eve were punished, too. Were they to blame? Yes, terribly so. Why? Because the serpent could not have forced them to sin. He could only whisper to them bad thoughts—that the forbidden fruit was nice; and that it was unkind of God to forbid it; that what God said was not true, etc. Were they awfully ashamed of their wickedness? How do you know? (*v.* 8). They might well be. Think how very good God had been to them. Spent thousands and thousands of years making the earth, and the sea, and the trees and flowers, and animals, all for sake of man; made man after His own likeness. And then to treat Him like that after all! And to let that sneaking serpent, God's enemy, trick them into doing it!

Now, some people think that this story is meant to be an exactly literal account of the way Adam and Eve sinned; that there was really a serpent talking, and the two trees with the curious names. And other people think that while it is meant to be a true account of the sin of our first parents, it is told in a sort of parable form, like "The Prodigal Son," or "The Siege of Mansoul"—that the serpent and the trees are but parables and pictures of greater things. We may not be perfectly sure from the Bible account which is the true notion—and it does not matter in the least. The meaning is perfectly clear in either case, that early man, by wilfully choosing sin, by trying what sin was like, brought sin into this world. How does it concern us? Does God punish you and me for something that Adam and Eve did thousands of years ago? Certainly not. And yet every child in this class has a close concern with this sin of Adam and Eve. How? It brought wrong-doing into this world, that God had made so beautiful; and it has made it harder to this day for any of us to be good. Try to understand this.

§ 3. Why Temptation Allowed to Come

When God had breathed into our first parents the breath of life, and they found themselves here in His lovely world, what sort of character had they? It was *innocence* like that of a little baby who does not know anything about evil, and has not ever had to choose between good and evil. Which is the higher sort of goodness: the *innocence* of the baby who does not know about evil, and has never been tempted, or the strong, brave *righteousness* of a noble woman or man who does know about evil, and has been tempted by evil, but who, by God's grace, has bravely conquered, and refused to do the evil? Which is the higher, and braver, and stronger? Which does God most value— *Innocence* or *Righteousness*? So every innocent baby must one day come to the "knowledge of good and evil." He must see the good and the evil, and deliberately choose; otherwise his innocence is of little value. That is the use of temptation. Every temptation to temper, or laziness, or disobedience, or any sin, is like a call from God, saying: Choose between good and evil. That is the way that God makes character. By the "knowledge of good and evil," and deliberately choosing the good, righteousness, nobleness of character, is formed, which God so values. Therefore Adam and Eve had to be tested—tried. They had a fair, beautiful start in life, with no knowledge of evil—holy innocence, no taint of sin. But it was still only *Innocence*, and God wanted *Righteousness* (i.e., *Innocence preserved in the presence of temptation*). Therefore, the "knowledge of good and evil" had to come to them; and so, in this wonderful old-world picture, we see the man and woman in the Garden of Delight with everything, it would seem, to keep them in union with God for ever.

And then we see the testing. There stands before them this mystic "tree of the knowledge of good and evil;" and God forces their attention to it by a command that they should not eat of it. They must only know evil by looking at it, not by sharing in it. They must know it in the way that God Himself knows it—as a possible thing, but a hateful thing. In the presence of that tree and that command the old childlike *innocence* must change either into a higher thing or a lower. Can you explain that? They have now a choice; they must obey or disobey; do good or do evil; and so the knowledge of good and evil has come. Conscience has begun to act. If they can resist this temptation, they will rise up into the path of righteousness of life—into a noble condition of moral manhood.

§ 4. *The Tempter*

Now God is watching His new creatures to see what they will do. He has spent thousands of years in

48

preparing for this moment. Do they love Him enough to do what He asks, or will they give Him deepest pain by yielding? Perhaps they might have conquered if no enemy near. But they have a terrible enemy. Who is it? He was once an angel of God; but when his testing-time came, as it comes to all, he "abode not in the truth" (John viii. 44). He rebelled against God, and other angels rebelled with him (Jude, *v.* 6). And now he is miserable and angry, and wants to drag everybody else down. So in our picture we see next a creeping, cunning, crawling serpent—a horrible, uncanny thing that could creep through any hole, and twine around one, where an open enemy could be kept out. What is meant by the serpent? (Revelation xii. 9). How does he conquer? By power and strength? No (*v.* 13); beguiled, just as in story of *Mansoul.* It is this old story in the Bible that taught the writer of "The Siege of Mansoul" how to represent the devil.

Tell me how he lied and deceived? Yes. What did Eve do? Did she run away, or get angry with him? No; stood and listened, and looked, and the more she looked the nicer it seemed to eat of the tree. What does *v.* 6 say? What does this mean? That sin, before it is done, seems often pleasant to people; that is why they do it; and if they keep on thinking how nice it is, they will very likely do it. They must resist at once or flee from the temptation.

And so at last—oh! the misery, and shame, and horror of it!—Eve reached forth, and broke the good, loving God's command, and then she got Adam to do the same, and so they were both in rebellion; and so the cunning devil had triumphed, and God was sorrowful and disappointed, and in that moment "sin entered into the world, and death by sin."

§ 5. *Original Sin*

Does it matter to us that the first of our race turned to wrong instead of right? How? Does God punish us for what a man and woman did many thousands of years ago? Certainly not. But the evil thing got "into our blood," as people say. You know how people notice that there is a likeness between parents and children; a likeness in appearance; a likeness in character and ways also.

Sometimes people say when a boy has a bad temper, or a cowardly spirit, or some mean little tricks, "Oh! he inherited that from his grandfather, or father, or some ancestor of his." That is an awful thing, but it is true. Character is handed down like that. And so the badness got into our race; and it is harder for us to be good now, and easier to be evil, because mankind, at the beginning, did wrong, and kept on doing it. (This is what the Church means by doctrine of original sin.)

Now, do you know why this story is so very real to us? Because that very thing is frequently happening to us all. God wants us all to rise to *Righteousness*. (Give definition of it.) Has the "knowledge of good and evil" come to any of you? Have you sometimes chosen the good—sometimes the evil? Will you remember next time how solemn these choices are, and that God is watching, as long ago in Eden—lovingly watching for you to conquer, and standing by to help you? And if you fail, and the great shame and sorrow come, and you hear a still small voice inside you asking, "What hast thou done?" will you remember something like that told in the story (*v.* 8)? What did they do? Hide. Aye, just as you want to do when you have sinned; all the courage and the bright, glad confidence go out of your life, and you feel ashamed and degraded, and want to hide from God. Could they hide from God? Can anyone hide? No; better come right off and tell Him all; not make beggarly excuses like Adam and Eve.

§ 6. *The Deceiver and the Deliverer*

There are a great many lessons in this story—too many to mention. Just think of two.

1. The way in which this mean, slimy, crawling devil tries to cheat you. You remember how often he has done it; and how angry you were with him, and with yourself afterwards. Pray for more anger against him and against yourself, and more love to the good Father above whom we so continually disappoint.

2. A very touching lesson. This is the touching lesson: That when this man and woman had done the devil's bidding, and grieved and disappointed the good God; and when, in the shame of their sin, they felt no longer fit for God's eye—tried to cover their nakedness with a few leaves—then who was it provided a covering to clothe them, that they might venture to live in His presence without terror and degradation? Who? God Himself (*v.* 21). It shows that God was too kind, and

noble, and loving to keep His anger against them, or to banish them for ever. This is the lesson, that it is God Himself who relieves man's shame, and comforts him; and that if you are ashamed, and miserable, and afraid, on account of sin, God has taken care for you, as for Adam and Eve; that through the blood of Christ your iniquity should be forgiven, and your sin covered. Tell me the great promise of God in cursing the serpent (iii. 15). What does it mean? Seed of woman? Bruise his head? Bruise his heel? This is the loving promise. When men have disappointed and grieved God sorely, and must suffer what they have brought on themselves, God says, "I must go down to them, and not let them suffer alone. I must suffer for them myself, to undo their terrible evil." And so our Lord Jesus Christ was to come, who His own self bare our sins in His own body on the tree.

QUESTIONS FOR LESSON II

Tell story of the siege of Mansoul?

Tell story of Adam and Eve and the Serpent?

Names of the two trees?

Who was first tempted?

Whom did she tempt?

What do you think the whole story means?

What good use have temptations?

CAIN AND ABEL

Ch. IV. and V. 21 to end

It is well to keep in view the relative importance of the different parts of the teaching. The three great subjects of this early history are The Creation, The Fall, and The Flood. This is a less important Lesson, but a very important one for all that. Man has been created. Man has fallen. The tendency to evil has come into the race; but it is not, therefore, necessary for man to be evil. Here we have the first representations of the *two great classes* into which all mankind has since divided—those who yield to the evil tendencies, and those who, for right and duty, and for God, fight against them.

§ 1. *The Two Boys*

Question briefly over last Lesson. Necessity of having a free choice; wrong choice made; fall into sin; banishment from Eden, etc. Now Adam and Eve in exile, saddened and troubled, lost the bright joyousness of the Paradise life. But were they utterly hopeless? Was God against them? Was He willing to forgive them?

Did He want them and their descendants to win back a high life still? What promise had He given? (*ch.* iii. 15). What did that mean? So there was hope for the future in spite of the sin.

Now what does first verse tell us? Birth of baby boy; delight of the mother. What did she say of it? I wonder if she thought that this was the promised Seed of the woman (iii. 15); that this baby boy should grow up noble and powerful, and bruise the head of Satan, who had tempted them to sin. What do you think? At any rate, she would probably feel, "Here is a new start; a new hope. This boy has not sinned like us. He will start clear as we did before the fall." Was it so? Ah, no. That is the awful thing about parents doing wrong. When they had done one sin, it led them to others, and the evil habit of sin came. And the terrible thing about sin is that what is in the parents descends to the children (give illustrations). And so that baby boy would not find it so easy to go right. Yet, in spite of that, could he have done well? How do you know? Yes, because God wanted to help him, and because his brother, born of same parents, *did* try to do well, and God accepted him.

Now think of the two brothers growing up, probably with several sisters. (Jews did not take much notice of birth of girls.) What sort of boys do you think they were? Guess? Can only guess by after-life. Cain, I think, a big dark fellow, sulky, jealous, passionate. Abel, with his faults, too, but trying to be good; a much more lovable boy; probably a greater favourite with parents and sisters, because of his being so lovable. Probably this would make Cain more sulky and jealous still. I dare say there was many a fight, and that Cain had struck blows with his fist often before he struck the blow with that heavy weapon that killed his brother. Murder, and robbery, and drunkenness, and every great evil is of gradual growth. (Warn children about giving way to ill-temper. By giving way the temper grows strong and evil, and you can never trust yourself. When impulse comes to strike or to speak angrily, remember, "Here is the devil coming to me as to Cain. He shan't conquer me. God will help me." I know of a boy in such case who ran off to his room to fight it out alone with God's help. It is a great strength and gladness to you when you conquer, and it is a shame and a contemptible thing to be beaten by the great enemy when you need not be.)

As they grew up they were put to work. That is God's will for us all. What trades? So now we think of them as two sturdy young men, brown and healthy, a shepherd and a gardener. Out at work in the fields all day, coming back to their family at night. And still the two separate natures were growing—the sulky one growing sulkier, the lovable one growing more lovable. Poor Eve must have been disappointed as she thought of all her high hopes for her eldest boy. Here is the beginning of the great division of GOOD and BAD people in the world. Was there any religion then? Any worship? (*vv.* 3, 4). Parents must have taught the family about God. How was God to be worshipped then? By offerings. How is He to be worshipped now? Just the same. We pray to God when we want His help; but no real acceptable worship unless by offering to give our efforts, our influence, ourselves for His service. Emphasize the fact that religion is the merest mockery without offering our lives to God.

§ 2. *The Murder of Abel*

Tell me about offerings and result. Why do you think God accepted one and rejected the other? (Hebrews xi. 4). By *faith*, i.e., Abel believed in God and trusted Him, and felt Him always present, and his offering was expression of love and gratitude to Him. Cain, it would seem, had no such feelings. Perhaps he thought he could manage his fruits very well without God, and so saw nothing to thank Him for. How did Cain bear rejection? Ah, jealousy and spite are terrible things to grow. What *ought* Cain have felt? "Must be something wrong in me. O God, help me to find it out, and get rid of it, that I may be pleasing to Thee."

So for days and days he went about fierce and sulky, and threatening Abel. How did God deal with him? (*vv.* 6, 7). Don't you think God was very good to him? God spoke to him through conscience as He speaks to you. Instead of punishing, He pleads with him and asks him to be reasonable. God says: "It is not my fault that you are rejected. I must reject evil. I don't like to reject you. I want to bless you, and make you good. Now turn to me, and I will help you to be good, and then I can bless you like Abel. But if you don't, sin lieth—i.e. croucheth—at the door, like a wild beast ready to destroy you." Could God have done more for him? So when you, too, are cross or sulky, or wicked in any way, think of God looking on you kindly as on

Cain, and trying to reason with you by your conscience, and save you.

Did God prevail with him? No; sulkiness and hatred grew and grew till one awful day something happened that probably Cain never thought would happen. What? Think of him, with his pointed wooden spade, digging; Abel is passing; a few words between them; suddenly, his eyes blazing with rage, he whirls the heavy implement over his head, and brings it down crash on Abel's skull. And then, oh, the awful horror! Abel lying in his blood, with dead, white face looking up to God, and Cain flying from the horror of it—anywhere—anywhere. No use; that dead face and staring eyes will never leave his memory, wherever he flies to. That is his curse for ever. That "curse of Cain," ever since, has fallen on every murderer. (Illustrate, e.g., *Dream of Eugene Aram*, life-terror of Charles IX. of France after massacre of St. Bartholomew.) Probably did not intend to kill him. That is the awfulness of sin, and especially of jealousy and ill-temper; men do what they did not mean to do just before, and curse themselves for ever.

§ 3. The Pain of Conscience

There was One whom Cain could not escape. What did God demand? Think of his terror, perhaps in the dark night, hiding from God and man. Perhaps a voice that he could hear; perhaps cry in his conscience within, "What hast thou done?" Oh, it is awful to have to hear God's voice when we are going against Him. Do people hear it still? How? Did you ever hear conscience? Did

Cain tell the truth? Could he hide it from God? What did God say? (*v.* 10). Meaning of blood crying to God?

What was Cain's punishment? (*vv.* 10-14). But there was a worse punishment which he must always carry with him? Yes; the agony of his remorseful conscience; the blood crying to God. Bad enough to be a fugitive and vagabond, driven away from home, afraid of being murdered. But these not the worst. By-and-by new home; where? (*v.* 16). Son born; who? By-and-by, too, God protected him from being murdered (*v.* 15). But do you think he was therefore happy? I can imagine the fierce, heart-broken man throwing himself on the desert ground, maddened with the thought of his murdered brother. I can imagine him with the horrid vision of the dead face bringing out the sweat on him in the darkness of the midnight. Always he must hear the voice of his brother's blood crying to God; always he must feel God's severest torture in conscience. For God is very stern and awful when people insist on going wrong. He spares them no pang of that agony of conscience. Why? Because He is revengeful? To please Himself? No; but to try if anything will bring them back to the Father who loves them.

I wonder if God's love prevailed this time with Cain. No one can tell. Perhaps he repented; perhaps we shall meet him some day in God's kingdom, and hear him tell of another "voice of a brother's blood" (Hebrews xii. 24) of which, perhaps, he has since learned. What did Abel's blood cry to God for? Vengeance. What does Christ's Blood cry to God for? He laid down His life, and shed His Blood, that we might be pardoned.

"Abel's blood for vengeance
Calleth to the skies;
But the blood of Jesus
For our pardon cries."

Do you think God will hear the cry of that Blood? For every poor sinner? Even if as bad as Cain? Yes; the worst sinner can kneel down in his penitence at God's feet, and be forgiven through that precious Blood.

§ 4. Good Men and Bad Men

So the world grew on for hundreds and hundreds of years, very clever and wise, inventing what? (iv. 20, 21, 22). But clever and wise without God (read *ch.* vi. 5). What an awful disappointment to God, who made men in His image. Were any good amongst them all? Who? (iv. 26; v. 22-24). Who in v. 29? Yes; Noah. This brings us down near to the story of the Flood, in next lesson.

QUESTIONS FOR LESSON III

Who were Cain and Abel?

What were their characters?

Could Cain be good if he wanted? Did God say anything to help him?

What was his punishment?

What do you think was his worst punishment? Did his conscience hurt him? Does yours sometimes?

THE FLOOD

Lecture to the Teacher

I

I have already pointed out to you the existence of what we might almost call a "Bible before the Bible"—a series of histories now lost to the world, which were probably God's guide to mankind in primitive times, and parts of which have been, by God's "inspiration of selection," chosen by the inspired writers to be handed down to us incorporated in our Holy Scriptures. The oldest of them all are the Creation story and the Deluge story—probably existing in the primeval world, and handed down by word of mouth from father to son, the only approach to a Bible which they possessed. We have already referred to the Creation story; and now we have before us the ancient Deluge story, which must have been told over and over again by Noah and by Shem to their descendants, and which may probably have been brought by Abraham from Ur of the Chaldees.

All we know is that the old story was probably one of the national treasures long before the Book of

Genesis was written, helping to keep religion alive while Israel was in Egyptian slavery; and it sets one's thoughts away far back in the primeval days, when men in the original cradle of the race told it to each other as a divine teaching, and, as they separated into many lands, carried the old story with them, frequently corrupting it much in its transmission.

Most of the early races of the world had traces of a story of the Deluge as well as of Creation, with so much resemblance between them that it seems probable that they were derived from some original source far back in the ages, perhaps in the cradle of the human race by the Mediterranean Sea. Some scholars tell us that the present Mediterranean Sea was anciently a fertile, thickly peopled valley until the Atlantic broke in at the Straits of Gibraltar and swept over it all. At any rate, it is an extraordinary fact that such similar accounts should exist. Rationalistic writers say they are all myths; and they add that since the Hebrew story is like them, it is, probably, also a myth. "But how explain the fact that, in all parts of the world, people have stumbled on the same myth? What is there, apart from tradition, that commends to the imagination and invention of men the fable of a Deluge, and the saving of one household in an ark?" Then look at the similarity. The Persian tradition tells that the ark was landed on a northern mountain. The Phrygian account is confirmed by a medal on which is depicted an ark floating on the waters, with people within; a bird is perched on the top, and another flies towards it with a branch in its mouth. With the Creation story which George Smith found in the Nineveh tablets

fifty years ago was a Deluge story in the ancient writing
of Chaldea. The reader can judge of its resemblance to
the Bible narrative by the extracts given below.[1] Surely

[1]I give here extracts from the Chaldean epic, emphasizing by
italics its resemblances to the Scripture account, and also the
parts which, in their gross polytheism, contrast most strikingly
with the pure, majestic presentation of God in the Bible:—

The city of Surippak, which as thou knowest,
Is built (on the bank of) the Euphrates.
This city was (already) old when the gods within it
Set their hearts to cause a flood, even the great gods
(As many as) exist, Anu the father of them,
The warrior Bel their prince,
Bir their throne-bearer, En-migi (Hades) their chief.
  . . . .

O man of Surippak, son of Ubara-Tutu,
Frame the house, build a ship: leave what thou canst;
Resign (thy) goods, and cause thy soul to live,
And bring all the seed of life into the midst of the ship.
As for the ship which thou shalt build,
 . . . cubits shall be in measurement its length;
And . . . cubits the extent of its breadth and its height;
Into the deep (then) launch it.
  . . . .

He speaks to Ea (his) lord:
'(O my lord) none has ever made a ship (on this wise)
That it should sail over the land! . . .
I fashioned its side and closed it in;
I built six stories (?); I divided it into seven parts;
Its interior I divided into nine parts.
I cut worked (?) timber within it.
I looked upon the rudder, and added what was lacking.
I poured 6 sars of pitch over the outside;
(I poured) 3 sars of bitumen over the inside;
3 sars of oil did the men carry who brought it. . . .

I gave a sar of oil for the workmen to eat;
2 sars of oil the sailors stored away.
For the (workmen) I slaughtered oxen;
I killed (sheep) daily:

· · · · · · · · · · · · · ·

With all I had I filled it; with all I possessed I filled it;
With all the gold I possessed I filled it;
With all that I possessed of the seed of life of all kinds I filled it.
I brought into the ship all my slaves and my handmaids,
The cattle of the field, the beasts of the field, the sons of my people
    did I bring into it.
The sun-god appointed the time and
Utters the oracle: "In the night will I cause the heavens
To rain destruction;
Enter the ship and close the door!"
I entered into the ship and closed my door.
When I had closed the ship, to Buzar-sadi-rabi the sailor
I entrusted the palace with all its goods.
Mu-seri-ina-namari (the waters of the morning at dawn)
Arose from the horizon of heaven a black cloud;
The storm-god Rimmon thundered in its midst, and
Nebo and Merodach, the king, marched in front;
The throne-bearers marched over mountain and plain;
The mighty god of death lets loose the whirlwind.
Bir marches, causing the storm (?) to descend;
The spirits of the under-world lifted up (their) torches;
With the lightning of them they set on fire the world;
The violence of the storm-god reached to heaven;
All that was light was turned to (darkness).
In the earth like · · · (men) perished (?)

· · · · · · · · · · · · · · ·

· · · · · · · · · In the heaven
The gods feared the deluge, and
Hastened to ascend to the heaven of Anu.
The gods cowered like a dog who lies in a kennel.

64

the widespread tradition of the Flood is intelligible only
on the belief that such an event did occur; an event so

Istar cried like a woman in travail.

.   .   .   .

I beheld the deep, and uttered a cry,
For the whole of mankind was turned to clay;
Like trunks of trees did the bodies float.
I opened the window, and the light fell upon my face;
I stooped, and sat down weeping;
Over my face ran tears.
I beheld a shore beyond the sea;
Twelve times distant rose a land.
On the mountains of Nigar the ship grounded;
The mountain of the country of Nigar held the ship, and allowed
    it not to float,
One day, and a second day did the mountain of Nigar hold it;
A third day, and a fourth day, did the mountain of Nigar hold it;
A fifth day, and a sixth day, did the mountain of Nigar hold it.
When the seventh day came I sent forth a dove, and let it go.
The dove went and returned; a resting-place it found not,
    and it returned.
I sent forth a swallow, and let it go; the swallow went
    and returned;
A resting-place it found not, and it turned back.
I sent forth a raven, and let it go;
The raven went and saw the going down of the waters; and
It approached, it waded, it croaked, and did not turn back.
Then I sent forth (everything) to the four points of compass;
    I offered sacrifices.
I built an altar on the summit of the mountain.
I set libation-vases seven by seven;
Beneath them I piled up reeds, cedar wood and herbs.
The gods smelt the savour; the gods smelt the sweet savour;
The gods gathered like flies over the sacrifice.'"

Sayce, Early Israel, Appendix II.

impressive as to be remembered and handed down through all the branches into which the race divided; an event simply and truly related in Genesis, but variously distorted in the heathen races.

I do not desire to dogmatize about it. At any rate, here we have one ancient account of the Deluge—pure, simple, lofty, religious, and a number of other accounts, marked by polytheism and silly, degrading superstition; and the question comes again, as in the Creation story, Is there any way of accounting for the difference, except by a belief in inspiration?

II

Be careful to dwell especially on the *moral* teaching of this Lesson. The details about the numbers of animals, the size of the ark, the extent of the Deluge, etc., are interesting; but do not spend much time on them. Keep them subordinate to the main purpose. The minute knowledge of these things does not help much to make people "wise unto salvation." Keep in mind that the story of the Flood was given to help to make us better men, and for that purpose the child's attention must be kept not so much on the Flood as on the God who sent the Flood.

Get your own mind thoroughly impressed by the lesson of the story—THAT THERE IS NOTHING TOO GREAT OR TOO TERRIBLE FOR GOD TO DO FOR THE SAKE OF RIGHTEOUSNESS. It seemed to Him worth while to spend thousands of years in preparing this world as a stage or platform for man to work out his destiny, and grow towards righteousness; and now it seems worth destroying the world—aye, or fifty worlds—rather than let iniquity overcome righteousness. So intense is the Divine earnestness for good and against evil. You might go on from this to refer to that highest proof of all of what God would do for this purpose, and point them to that awful sight of Christ upon the cross. There is no more important lesson for the children than this of the intensity of God's hatred of evil, and the intensity of God's desire for righteousness in us. He hesitates not to bring suffering and pain on men if it be necessary. He hesitates not to bring suffering and pain on Himself, so intensely does He love righteousness and hate iniquity. The Christian world is growing too tolerant of evil now. Try to teach the *intensity* of God's hatred of evil and God's desire for good.

LESSON ON THE FLOOD

Ch. VI. v. 9 to end, and VII.

COMMENTARY

VI. 3. "120 years," i.e., until the Flood should destroy them.

V. 6. "Repented." See note on *ch.* v. 8.

VII. 19. This at first sight seems to indicate universal Deluge. But remember the Deluge is described from point of view of an eye-witness, not from that of Omniscience. This is how it would appear to a man in the Ark. Some people think the Deluge only partial, and say that, as God's purpose was only to sweep away the sinful race of man, a flooding of that portion which was the cradle of the race would have been sufficient. This matter is of no practical importance to us, and we can never decide it. To say that this verse decides it is to forget the similar expressions.—Deuteronomy ii. 25: Genesis xli. 57; 1 Kings xviii. 10, etc.

Better begin at *ch.* vi. 9. The previous verses bring up a difficult question, whether by the sons of God are meant fallen angels, from whom sprang the giants or Nephilim, in *v.* 4, or whether they are the sons of the godly race of Seth; see *ch.* iv. 26: "Then began men to call on name of the Lord." It is an interesting discussion, with great thinkers on either side. It contains valuable lessons for older people, but it may be omitted here.

§ 1. The Inhabitants of the Earth—State of Religion on Earth

It is now a long time since Creation and Fall. Thousands of years, probably, of human life. How are they progressing? Getting better? Repenting of the Fall? Ah, no. They have got richer and more civilized (*last Lesson*)—tools, and musical instruments, and cities, and a good deal of progress of that kind. Does God care for all that? Yes, certainly. It is His will for the world. But is it the chief thing? What is? Yes; righteousness. Oh, if He could only get them to be good! That is the one supreme desire of His heart. What a great deal of pain and disappointment must come to God!

What is the account of these people for whom He had made the world? (*vv.* 5, 6, 7, 11, 12). *Repented* (*v.* 6); not mean that God saw He had made a mistake— but a way of expressing strongly God's great sorrow and anger. Was everybody evil? (*v.* 8). What a grand thing to see one family standing alone for God in the midst of this awful evil. So one schoolboy, one man or woman now—a sight dear to God. Noah is called in 2 Peter ii. 5, a "preacher of righteousness." Probably he preached much to those wicked people about God; but there is a better sort of preaching than merely saying something. What? *Being* something. What was Noah? (*v.* 9). It is not talking that is important in the world; but what? *Being.* What is the greatest thing any man can do for salvation of the world? Preach? Talk? No. *To be* a good man himself. There are a great many wants to be supplied in the world; but the greatest want is this: good men and women, good boys and girls, who, in the quiet, silent beauty of a noble life, are making people love religion. That is the greatest help Noah could give to God, and the greatest help you can give.

Through all the pain and disappointment wicked men caused Him, God was very patient, hoping for some repentance. Now at last things were so bad, that righteousness was nearly trampled out; only one family remained. So God could wait no longer. What did He decide? (*v.* 13). Things had all gone wrong. The world must get a new start. Was not it an awful thing to drown thousands of people? Yes. But it was far better to have them drowned than to have them corrupting each other more. God's hatred of wickedness is so awful; His longing for righteousness is so intense. He thinks even to make or destroy a whole world is not too much to crush out wickedness and help on righteousness. All this fearful Flood is for the sake of destroying wickedness. All this plan about the Ark, for sake of saving the seed of righteousness. Should it not teach us the grandeur of being good, the horribleness of being evil, when they seem so awfully important in God's sight?

§ 2. The Building of the Ark

Now tell me about the directions for the Ark? Who and what were to be saved in it? Was the wicked world to get any more chance of repentance? (*v.* 3). Yes. So Noah was to spend all these years in warning, preaching, and building the ark. Now, a curious sight; a great field without hedges or walls; men cutting down trees, and preparing for the great shipbuilding. A curious place to build a ship in a field, no water near. Imagine the people coming in the evening to laugh and jest about it: "That poor old fool Noah—he has been bothering us with his preachings all these years, and now he has gone quite mad; come and see him building a boat in the middle of a field;" and again Noah would plead with them: "Oh, don't force God to destroy you. Tell Him you are sorry, and pray to Him to forgive you." And they would laugh more than ever. Even Noah's carpenters (I suppose he employed carpenters) did not believe or care about God. How terrible; the very men that were building the ark would be destroyed themselves. And so the years went on. The boys that used to laugh at Noah's

70

Ark were grown to be men. The 120 years were nearly expired; and still the beautiful sunny weather, and no sign of the Flood. And they were more convinced than ever that Noah was a very great fool.

§ 3. *The Flood*

Now begins *ch.* vii. 120 years after *ch.* vi. Suddenly one day an order came to Noah. What? (*ch.* vii. 1-4). Now he knew the time was near—only seven days. Now the people are coming in greater crowds to look. The ark is finished, and all the day beasts and birds in pairs are being gathered in, and Noah and his family are busy from morning till night storing provisions.

I wonder did he preach more earnestly; or was he too busy to preach now. I can fancy the people laughing louder than ever to hide the little feeling of uneasiness beginning to arise, and the women sometimes crying secretly at home in fear for their little children; but nobody daring to show their fear, and a general determination to carry it off with a high hand, and defy God and Noah by plunging into worse wickedness; and still all the week, the beautiful summer, and the hot sun overhead, and the lovely fields and flowers. Five days over. Six days. Clear blue sky still. After mocking Noah till they are tired, they all go to bed that sixth night, a little uneasy, perhaps; the sky is darker, the wind is rising, but that has often been before. But at midnight the terror begins. The houses are rocking in the storm; the deafening thunder, the lightning in great sheets, making all clear as noonday; and oh, the awful, awful rain! Not drops, not showers, but great sheets of water; "the fountains of the great deep were broken up, and the windows of heaven were opened." Before morning the water was in about their feet. Still they hoped; often saw great storm before; will be over to-morrow. But to-morrow it was worse, and next day, and next, and the water was up to their knees, to their waists, and still rain, rain, rain! hopeless, unceasing, overwhelming. They could see the great ark through the storm beginning to float; but God had shut in Noah (*v.* 16), and they had shut themselves out. Too late now! So they rush out in wild terror, and the men and women climb the trees, and rush up the hills with their children; but slowly, steadily, remorselessly, the water creeps up. Let us drop the story; it is too horrible. The darkness settled down over the fierce, wild wash of waters, and in the morning the whole country is drowned; only the ark floating on the waters contains any life. Read *vv.* 18-24.

§ 4. The Ark of Christ's Church

What is the meaning of the expression, "The Ark of Christ's Church"? Explain? Yes. God's great hatred of sin is still the same. But God's love and desire to save are also the same. If men repented of their sin, and came to Noah's Ark, do you think they would have been cast out? How is this like the Ark of the Church?

So there is something to add to this awful lesson of God's anger against sin at the Flood, that we may understand that it is not only a just but also a loving anger; that He destroyed men's bodies to keep them from destroying men's souls; that while He hesitated not to let men suffer terribly in His intense earnestness about sin, He hesitated not to make Himself suffer terribly too. Look at the bleeding, tortured, dying Man hanging upon the Cross of Calvary two thousand years after, and remember that was God Himself, who had thought it worth while to destroy a world to put away sin, and who now thought it worth while to come down and bleed, and suffer, and die Himself, that there might be this "Ark of Christ's Church" for sinful, penitent men.

> "Glory be to Jesus,
>   Who, in bitter pains,
> Poured for me the life-blood
>   From His sacred veins!

> "Grace and life eternal
>   In that blood I find;
> Blest be His compassion,
>   Infinitely kind!"

QUESTIONS FOR LESSON IV

What sort of world was it before Flood?

Why was the Flood sent?

Was everyone to be destroyed?

Name Noah's three sons.

What did Noah do to save the people before Flood?

What two things about God are here taught?

LESSON V

AFTER THE FLOOD

Ch. VIII. and IX. to v. 20

§ 1. A New World

Last Lesson was about what? (Question so as to bring out the lesson of God's intense earnestness about righteousness and sin. So awful and evil is sin that it was worth destroying the whole world rather than let evil conquer.)

We left Noah and his family tossing about on the heaving flood, and all the world drowned; corpses floating past—of men and animals, etc. Think of the awful creepy feeling of it—alone; no one else alive in the whole wide world; nothing to be seen but the grey sky and the pitiless rain, and the waters dotted with dead bodies. Perhaps those within could not see all this; but that would only intensify the horror in their imagination.

"Alone, alone, all, all alone—
Alone, on a wide, wide sea!

. . . .

The many men, so beautiful!
And they all dead did lie.

. . . .

I closed my eyes, and kept them close,
And the balls like pulses beat;
For the sky and the sea, and the sea and the sky,
Lay like a load on my weary eye,
And the dead were at my feet."

And so the weary weeks and months went on. Then came the wind assuaging the waters, the pointed mountain-tops appearing; at last, one night, a creaking, grinding noise, and a bumping on a ridge of rock, and then the great ark settling down at last on one of the mountains of Ararat. Day after day the world rose gradually out of its grave of waters. But Noah could not see; could only guess; probably window only in roof (vi. 16, R.V.; viii. 13). How find out? And then? (*v.* 8). Any boy that keeps pigeons would understand the tenderness of Noah in *v.* 9. Next time dove sent forth again; what sign did she bring? Still they could only guess. Imagine the impatience to look out! Imagine eager excitement the day Noah was to take off the cover, and they could see—what? Behold, the whole face of the earth was dry—a new, clean world, all washed and bright and beautiful, with the sun shining out behind the rain-clouds, and a lovely rainbow arching over the whole world from one side to the other. But not a man, woman, or child alive except themselves. Like a new Adam and Eve in a new world, Noah and his wife went forth with their family into this new world. First thing they did? (*v.* 20). Was God pleased? Like a family in our day, coming together at family prayers to thank God for the blessings of the day and His care of them. Does it please God? Yes (*v.* 21). God's great sorrow is through men's forgetting Him, and forgetting the beautiful life that He intends for them.

Now we have the new life beginning in the new world. Let us see God's promises and directions: (1) About the harvest? (viii. 22); (2) about the animals—what? (*v.* 2). Think what life would be but for that. If the horses and cows, and dogs and cats should cease to fear, and turn to attack us. Even the largest animals have the fear and dread on them. God has made us, so far, superior. How? (ii. 7). (3) Direction about blood. Why? To teach sacredness of life. All the wise men in the world cannot produce the tiniest life of plant or insect. God has kept all that entirely in His hands. Therefore life is sacred. (See in Mosaic ritual, Leviticus iii. 17; vii. 27; xvii. 10, etc.). But especially man's life. Why? (*v.* 6). Yes; man is in close relation with God. God's nature is in him; the divine conscience, with the consciousness of God and the eternal rule of right stamped on it. His life is most sacred of all. No man must take his own life or another's. God alone can give or take this great gift. So God appointed men themselves to guard man's sacred life, and to avenge all murder.

§ 2. Fresh Starts in Life

So God gave mankind a fresh start in life. If they would now try to be good and follow Him, all would be well. Does He give fresh starts now? Boys and girls got first good start at Baptism; received into Christ's Church. Do all keep faithful? When, after all God's goodness, they sin and forget Him, does He cast them out? What does He do? Gives new fresh start again and again when they come back sorrowfully to Him.

That is the happiness of belonging to God. "It is never too late to mend." No matter how bad the past, He will forgive. Does it matter much then about doing wrong? Are we just as well off as if we had not done it? No; for, first, we have pained and disappointed God; and, secondly, every time we go wrong it becomes harder to go right. God forgives us, and lovingly gives us the best fresh start He can. He cannot give us as good as before we did wrong; but He gives the best He can, and then the next best, and the next, while any chance of good remains.

But what of all the crowd of dead people that lay in the fields, and on the mountain-sides after the Flood? Ah, we know not. God had warned them, and given Noah many years to teach them. Perhaps they had had all their chance. If no further hope for them, who would be most sorry? God? Yes; if a sinner is lost, the worst pain is not to him, but to God. And if there be any possible chance of saving him, God will keep trying to save him. Do you think God forgot all about them now that they were dead? Do you think your father or mother would forget you in such case? There is a very curious, interesting passage (1 Peter iii. 18-20) where St. Peter is telling of our Lord's descent into Hades; and many think it means that our Lord, who had never forgotten them, went down to these poor outcasts to preach to them of a new hope and a fresh start for them through the coming of a Saviour. If that be really the meaning, does it not show us still more the boundlessness of God's great love?

§ 3. The Rainbow

Thus is the new world sent forth, and it begins with a beautiful sign of God's presence and promise. What? (*v.* 13). Most probably the rainbow had existed before, and that God directed Noah to look up to it now, and take it as a reminder of His promise for ever, just as the familiar rite of Baptism and the substances of bread and wine were made signs of Christ's new covenant.

Can you see anything in rainbow to remind us of God? (1) Bright, beautiful, hopeful; (2) spreads across whole visible sky; (3) stretches between heaven and earth; (4) made by light shining on dark rain-clouds, like a parable of the love shining through the gloom and anger, etc.

Another question about it. Who sent rainbow? Who sent the terrible storm and deluge? Yes, light and darkness, storm and sunshine, joy and sorrow, are not from different gods, as the heathen think. God sends all as are best for men. Would continual rainbows and promises do for the world? No; it needed also threatening, and deluge, and death. Would continual sunshine do for a plant? No, it needs sometimes sunshine, sometimes rain, sometimes fierce winds and storms. So with our lives. You would like all gladness; can't understand old age, and pain, and loneliness, and sorrow. You will by-and-by. You see God's one great longing for men is not merely to make them happy—but what? Yes; good. Because goodness and nobleness are far more precious than happiness. So He often lets a boy suffer pain or humiliation, and a rich man suffer loss, and all of us suffer hard work and discipline—why? Yes; to make us good at any cost. Always remember, then, that God's good hand is over all, and that He is trying in every way to help us to Himself.

QUESTIONS FOR LESSON V

Where did the Ark go aground?

What did Noah do to find out if the waters were abated?

What was God's sign of hope in the sky?

Noah's thanksgiving to God? (viii. 20).

What punishment directed about murder?

God's promise about harvests?

THE CALL OF ABRAHAM

Ch. XI. to v. 10, v. 26 to end, and XII.

(Cf. Acts VII. 1-6)

Note the two chief lessons: (1) Abram but a sinful man like us struggling to be good; (2) God is everywhere and at all times seeking for men whom He can use to help the world upwards.

Briefly remind of last Lesson. New, fresh start for humanity—rainbow, emblem of new hope before them, etc. Now, how had this hope been fulfilled? Tell me story of Babel. Our history keeps still in the valleys, the cradle of our race, where Noah's descendants were becoming great and powerful. Babel story seems to show that they were again displeasing God? What was He going to do now? Another flood? No (*ch.* ix. 11). Quite another plan. What? Separate a religious family to grow into a religious nation to keep alive religion in the world. This nation to be minded, and blessed, and punished, and helped, and watched over above all nations on earth. For their own sake? No; for sake of the world. What do you think of this plan? Henceforth the narrative concerns itself not with all humanity, but with God's chosen race, and those who affect their fortunes. Now think of God looking out over all the families on earth to choose the man for this purpose.

§ 1. The Shepherd Boy in Ur

A bright moonlight night in Ur, the holy city of the Chaldees, with its stately temple of the moon, crowded with worshippers, and outside the city the great spreading plains dotted over with brown tents, and flocks of sheep, and cows, and camels. The encampment of a shepherd clan under their chief Terah. Name some members of clan? (xi. 27-29). Notice especially Abram and Lot. Which the more important? Why? Yes, God had a great plan for Abram's life in the future. Brought up a shepherd boy, like what other great man? Think of quiet, thoughtful boy lying out at night on the plain, looking up at the brilliant moon and stars, and wondering about them. Did he know who made them? Perhaps primeval story of Creation and Flood were in his family; perhaps not.

At any rate, there was idol-worship in his home and false thoughts of God. See Joshua xxiv. 15; Genesis xxxi. 30. Probably the family went into the city with other Chaldeans to worship in temple of the moon. Do you remember something in Creation story that would have prevented this? (Genesis i. 16, Lesson I).

The Jewish Talmud pictures him turning from the Sun and Moon to some unknown God greater than they.

We may be sure that some such deep thoughts were stirring in the boy's heart—such thoughts as come to many of us in our better moments, when God's Spirit is near, and we realize that there is something within us more akin to God than to the grovelling world. By such thoughts God is always preparing boys and girls and men and women for high and useful future. The Jews have other old traditions about breaking his father's idols, and being tortured by Nimrod for his attacks on the national idolatry, etc. They all express what is true of the way in which loyal hearts in all ages are trained for their destiny by brave, honest faithfulness in the ordinary life at home and in business. God is always seeking boys and girls for high and useful futures, and training them as Abram was trained. God's great want now, as then, is fit men and women to help Him in blessing and ennobling the world. That is His constant work, and oh! He sorely needs help. Would He use you, do you think? If what? If want to be used and fitted. Does He need your help? Yes; the world is sorely in need of more true men and women, more nobleness, and earnestness, and enthusiasm, and quiet, loving self-sacrifice. God could use ten thousand times as many as He can now get. Should you like to help Him? Would not it be a grand ambition to help God; to be called by God, as Abram? Try to do your little part to make others happy and good in school, at home, wherever you are. Thus you are helping as a child, and preparing to be called of God to greater helpfulness by-and-by.

§ 2. God's Call

What was God's call? *Ch.* xii. 1. What was God's promise? (*v.* 2). "I will bless thee, and thou shalt be a blessing." God blesses people *in order that they may be a blessing.* God wants all his big family of mankind helped, and He blesses some with beauty, or loving hearts, or riches, or attractive manners, or, best of all, a deep sense of religion. Is it only for their own sake? Was Abram blessed for his own sake? Is not it beautiful, that plan of God blessing men and women that they may be a blessing to others?

How did God's call come? We don't know. Perhaps in a dream or some mysterious appearance to him; perhaps in a clear call of God and duty in his conscience, like as we get in our day, All we know is that he felt certain it was God's call, and unhesitatingly obeyed.

Why do you think this call came? Perhaps God had to take him away alone with Himself to train him; perhaps in his comfortable home he could not be trained for the great future. He must go out into unknown dangers and trials, and have to turn to God continually for help and comfort. Therefore, often God sends loneliness and sickness now. Perhaps, too, even if he kept himself holy in Ur, his children in the midst of idolatry would fall away, and so God's loving plan for the world be spoiled. We can only guess reason of call; but we know that God's reason was loving, and wise, and good.

Was it an easy call to obey? Would it be easy for a man comfortably settled in this country to go off at great risk and leave all his friends and relations to seek his fortune in a foreign land? Does God always ask only easy things? No; but, oh, He gives such blessedness and peace to those who follow Him, and the joy of His approval, which make up a thousand times over for the pain.

How far should the blessing, through Abram, extend? (v. 3). "All the families." How? Yes, by the Lord Jesus Christ coming. See greatness of God's plan. Not only raise up family and nation to help all about them, but, by-and-by, from that nation should Christ be born, to live and die for all men. Was it not worth while for Abram to bear the wrench of parting? And if, through you, God should be able to bless others, will it not be well worth while bearing something for it?

How did Abram respond to God's call? (compare ch. xi, 31, with Acts vii). He seems to have urged his father to move, and bring the whole family. Father must have been much attached to him, or would scarcely move. Who else went with him? But the enthusiasm of one could not do everything. Terah and Lot were half-hearted; got to Haran; fine, fertile fields; lovely country. "We will stay here, not go farther." Perhaps Abram grew slack, too, or perhaps could not leave the old father who loved him. At any rate, he stopped there, and the best years of his life were spent without doing what God wanted. When leave Haran? How old then? I think he was wrong in delaying in Haran. But as we don't know his reasons, and the Bible does not blame him, we must not. Perhaps like a young missionary resolving to go out, but not while father lived, and on his father's death going at once. At any rate, he never let go his purpose to do God's will as soon as he could. Picture Terah's death; funeral. Abram's preparation to start off again. Now a grave man of seventy-five years. Probably many arguments of his friends to detain him. His steadfast resolve for sake of God and right. Then the caravan starting in the early morning. Men of Haran wondering. "Other men, other caravans have gone to win riches and comfort. This man is going simply in obedience to God and his conscience." Would it not impress them with the reality of religion? So will you, too, impress men if your actions thus prompted.

§ 3. Bible Saints and Heroes

Question briefly on details to end of chapter xii., noticing that wherever he encamped he had an altar and family worship (*v.* 8).

Does God only call men because they are saints and heroes? Was Abram such? What is the sad story told of him in Egypt? Ah! he was no saint or hero; but he had in him the making of one, and God would make him one in time. God would not cast him away for one sin. People sometimes feel troubled at the Bible telling so openly the sins of its great men. Ought we to feel troubled? No; for not only is it an indication of the truthfulness of story which conceals nothing; but more than that—the story of these evils is a most valuable part of the lesson. We think of this Eastern shepherd as a hero; as quite different from other Easterners, to whom lying and crooked dealing were common. We do not expect him ever to act like them. We are shown at once our error. Abram is no hero, but a poor, sinful man, like ourselves, struggling to be good. We see that, unless helped by God's grace, he can be frightened and selfish, and tell lies like others of his race. And the lesson to be learned is this: See what religion did for this man. So grand became his faith that he is called "father of the faithful;" so noble his life that he is the "Friend of God." And the story is written of Abram's cowardice, and Jacob's treachery, and David's impurity, and the peevish quarrel of Barnabas and Saul, that we may see they are but like ourselves—plain, sinful men, struggling to be good, and that we may take courage that God will do for us what He did for them.

§ 4. God's Calls To-day

Is this the only call of God in history? No; only just one instance of the Divine call that comes to men in all the ages. Tell me any other in Bible? Moses, Joshua, Peter, Matthew, etc. Any in English or other history? Give instances, e.g., Tyndale called to go out into homeless exile, that England might be given the English Bible. Luther called from cloister, and friends, and companions to dare the mighty power of papal Rome. Were they called of God? Yes; we think so. By His clear voice in conscience; by the keen vision of duty.

Does He call simple people like us? Does God call men now as He did Abraham? Yes. Does He visibly appear and audibly call? How then? When we read the thrilling story of missions to the heathen; of men who gave up home and friends, and life itself, for God—when we see men and women going out to the lepers in India, risking the loathsome infection, that they may teach them the love of Christ—these are calls obeyed. And sometimes calls are disobeyed. Sometimes to young men and women, with no powerful home ties to detain them, comes the despairing cry from mission stations, "Come and help us; we are but one or two where there should be hundreds;" and conscience makes them uneasy, and whispers, "Go, get thee out from thy country," etc. Who is calling then? And sometimes they try to stifle God's voice, and stay lazily at home.

Is it only to heathen missions God calls? At home and abroad—everywhere—He is seeking men to help the world to be good; and some don't heed His call; settle down to grow selfish, and rich, and comfortable, with no higher aim than the oxen in the stall; and some say: "I hear the call; I will be a true man, God helping me. The world shall be some little bit the better of my being here. In home, or office, or shop, or wherever I am—whether I lose by it or not—God, and duty, and unselfishness, shall be my watchword for ever." God is calling us all to that grand life on earth, and, after that, to a life hereafter of still grander and blesseder possibilities of service.

QUESTIONS FOR LESSON VI

Meaning of "the call of Abram"?

Who called him and for what?

What sort of home had he and where?

How, do you think, did God's call come?

God's promise of a splendid future included others besides Abram himself? Lesson for us here?

"In thy seed shall all the families of the earth be blessed?" Explain.

Give other instances of God's call in history?

Are such calls to-day?

LESSON VII

LOT'S CHOICE

Ch. XIII., XIV., to v. 13

Chapter xiv. 1-13, may be read carefully and examined on so as to lessen next Sunday's work; but it will come better into next Lesson, with the exception of *v.* 12—Lot's capture. The main teaching of to-day is Lot's Choice, in *ch.* xiii.

Recapitulate last Lesson—Abram's call; such calls now. Abram's cowardice in Egypt—the one solitary sin recorded of him. Was he sorry for it? Where did he come to straight from Egypt; and what did he do? (xiii. 4). Does it not look like sorrow and new resolve, and asking God's help for the days to come? Do you think God forgave and helped him? Yes; he seems to have recovered all his greatness and nobleness of soul, and all through the rest of his life to have been a saint and hero.

§ 1. Lot's Character

We have to compare Abram to-day with a very

89

different man. Whom had he taken with him from Haran? (xii. 4). What relation? Whose son? Yes; took this orphan boy, son of his dead brother, helped him, trained him, shared his wealth with him. Did what generous uncles sometimes do for a dead brother's child now. I dare say the childless old man got fond of the boy. Probably Lot not very bad either. Was he religious? How do we know he had desires after right, and was vexed at wrong? (2 Peter ii. 7). I think he was a man who wanted to be good, and serve God. I don't think he could help wanting it. Why? Living in close companionship with one of the noblest souls on earth. It is a great privilege, but a great responsibility, to be placed with parents, friends, etc., nobler and more truly religious than ourselves. An old lady, dying, said to the writer once: "I have lived amongst the saints of the earth—lived, as servants say, 'in the very best families,' spiritually speaking, and I am little the better of it."

Was Lot much the better of it? What is our first opportunity of judging? Give me full account of the strife. Was it right for relations, households to fight? Money often causes it. Abram greatly grieved. Imagine him walking up the pasture slopes with Lot to talk it over. Then from the top sees whole country, the hills of the north, the rich, beautiful pastures of the south around Sodom, with the broad streams, where cattle could wade and drink. What offer does he make? What do our Lord and Apostles say about being unselfish and generous about other men's interests? (Matthew xx. 26; Romans xii. 10; Philippians ii. 4). How does Lot receive Abram's offer? What should he have said if he were a true-hearted man? "No, it is you who must choose. I owe you everything; the land is yours by God's promise. If we must part, you must choose." But no; he took advantage of his uncle's generosity, and so marked himself as a mean and ungenerous man.

Money a great test of character, "You never know a man till you have money dealings with him." Here are two men tested; which is the noble one? Which the mean one? Why? Abram knows that God has a grand plan for all men's lives, and that if he follow out God's plan for him, all will come right. What is God's plan for every life? To be true to one's ideals; to follow always the highest and most generous impulses; to "trust in God, and do the right." But suppose you lose money and position by so doing? Did Abram lose money here by so doing? Yes, certainly. Did Lot gain money by not following God's plan? Yes. Well, then, what should one do? Always follow the right and generous course, without calculating whether you gain or lose. God will, somehow, always make it right in the end.

Describe characters of the two men in a word: Abram, *spiritual;* Lot, *worldly.* Abram's highest aim? To follow God and duty. Lot's highest aim? To gain worldly advantage at any cost, though he would like to have religion too, if he would not lose by it. (Emphasize clearly this distinction.)

§ 2. A Life Mistake

Is it wrong to consider worldly interests in our decisions? Certainly not. What, then, was wrong with

Lot? That he considered nothing else; neglected the higher things for the lower. What did he gain? Money. Is anything more important than money? Happiness, character, religion, God's approval.

What did Lot lose? (1) What every man loses in character and happiness by doing anything wrong or ungenerous. It is a poor bargain to grow rich at the expense of your better nature. (2) Lost companionship of a man whose friendship would have helped him to be noble and happy. (3) Incurred terrible moral risk for his family. What is said of character of men of Sodom? (*v.* 13). Lot had a wife and several little daughters, and perhaps sons also. Sodom had rich pastures, and the town would be profitable market to sell milk and cattle, etc. But was it worth while for sake of this gain to let his children be brought up amongst wicked, immoral people? The greatest fool is the man who lives for this world only. Is similar mistake ever made now? Boy or girl looking out on life, north and south, like Lot, and choosing the situation and comradeship that lead to gain, or pleasure, or "good society," without ever thinking of usefulness, and character, and the approval of God. Parents who put children to a business that makes religion unlikely. Young person that marries, for wealth and position, one who is not truly a servant of God. They all usually gain the *lower* things that they aim at, but lose all the *higher*; and it is a miserable disappointment. Lot grew rich and prosperous; became a magistrate or town councillor in Sodom, and sat in the gate (*ch.* xix. 1), and married his daughters to men of Sodom, probably rich and prosperous men. He had all the success he aimed at. Was it a great success? Was he happy? (2 Peter ii. 8). Ah! poor Lot! He was disgusted with his new companions. His children got polluted by them, and became irreligious, and terrible misfortunes came on him, and his life ended in horror and misery; disgust with himself and his family. What does our Lord say of such gain? "What shall it profit a man?" etc.

§ 3. *The Power of a Servant of God*

Now let us compare Abram's life. A childless old man who had, I suppose, grown much attached to his nephew after all these years. He had lost, by his generosity, beautiful pastures. He was probably lonely, after Lot was gone. They were kinsmen parting in a foreign land.

But he had done the right; followed his high ideal; obeyed his noblest impulses; therefore, he could not be entirely unhappy. God always takes care of that. But God did more (*v.* 14, etc.). God is the unseen observer of all noble deeds; all such have His approval and reward. If you have Abram's faith, you will get Abram's happiness. How show similar faith? You, too, have high ideals, and generous, unselfish impulses. (Explain; give examples.) They come from God. Faith is shown by following them, like Abram, whether they lead to immediate gain or loss. You may have to give up some gain or pleasure; give up some unfit friend, and be lonely. Yet, if done in faith to please God, or to help men, God's blessing and peace will come to you as to Abram, and you will gain far more than you lost. (See Matthew xix. 20).

But see another great gain to servant of God. Influence. Boy proud to have influence over companions; grand power if used for good; great help in lifting men towards right. Which would have more influence: Abram or Lot? Young people sometimes told: "You must be close friends with careless, worldly people if you would do them good; not stand apart like a Pharisee," etc. What do you think? May you be friends with them? Yes; but never share in their evil pleasures, their disregard of Sunday, their wrong of any kind. If you would have influence with your companions, it is by their seeing your life truer and your ideals higher.

Look at Lot. Would he have influence? People of Sodom say: "That religion of Jehovah not much good if one of its holy men can come into our wicked city to make money." All his influence would be gone. He vexed his soul (2 Peter ii. 8), but did no good. See once when he tried to influence them. "Stand back," they cried; "this fellow wants to be a judge over us."

Look at Abram. Did he mix with men of Sodom? But did he care to do them good? Did he do them more good than Lot did? Yes: (1) fought and risked life for them; (2) pleaded eagerly with God (*ch.* xviii. 23) for them; (3) living out there on the heights, his holy life of faith must have been a great influence to make the men of Sodom ashamed of their wickedness. They could hardly forget how generous and unselfish he had been when they were captured. To have a strong influence for good is a great power to help the worldly and careless towards God. How can you have it? By associating with them in their pursuits, and being afraid to reprove

94

them? No. By being impertinent and conceited, and telling them how much better you are? No. By living close to the Lord Jesus; letting His spirit of helpfulness and unselfishness influence all your dealings with them; but never yielding up one jot of right, whether your action please or displease them.

QUESTIONS FOR LESSON VII

Who was Lot?

He treated Abram rather selfishly?

His choice led him into a dangerous place? How was it dangerous?

What did he gain and what did he lose by going there?

What happened to Sodom?

What happened to Lot?

ENCOURAGEMENT FOR ABRAM

Ch. XIV. v. 13, and XV.

Recapitulate last Lesson. Lot's choice; his mistake; contrast with Abram. Where was Abram when last mentioned? Where was Lot? *Toward* Sodom. I'm afraid he was now *in* Sodom. So men progress downward.

§ 1. Rescue of Lot

Now we have a great battle. Look at map. Valley of Jordan; important route between Egypt and Elam; great traffic, merchandise and passengers; like Suez Canal between India and England; great loss to England if enemy possessed it; ruin our trade. So with Chedorlaomer. This great warrior-king of Elam wanted this route clear, and all the tribes subject. How long remain subject? When rebel? What did he do? Name his tributary kings? All start off on campaign when season opened, to reconquer Jordan valley. Extraordinary campaign; curious tribes to conquer. Like Stanley's march through darkest Africa—big warrior nations; little forest dwarfs, four feet high, etc. First they conquered the Rephaim, ancient giants (refer to Og and his bedstead, Deuteronomy iii. 11); then the little brutish Horites, dwelling in caves in the ground. On through the Zuzims and Emims, till at last the army turn towards the powerful "Five Cities of the Plain." Name them and their kings. Which was Lot in? Give account of battle and result? So Lot did not gain much after all, even of the lower things, for which he bartered the higher.

Where was Abram? Was he injured by invaders? Read Psalms xci. 8. How did he hear of battle? What did he do? Had he much power and influence? Men of his character usually have. Three Canaanite chiefs who helped him? Why did he go? Yes, for Lot's sake. Lot had been mean and ungrateful, and gone to wicked Sodom. A lower type of man would say, Serve him right; why should I risk my life for him? But men like Abram are never kept back by such considerations from doing what is helpful and unselfish. Where did he get such disposition? Is that like God's own disposition? How shown? Yes, it was when we were mean, and wicked, and selfish that God loved us—that Christ died for us. Men touched with God's spirit must always act, in some little measure, like God. Tell me of expedition, and result? Daring thing to go and rescue Lot. Must, I think, have prayed to God about it, and then dared all, knowing he was acting rightly and unselfishly. Perhaps Isaiah refers to it (xli. 2, 3).

§ 2. *The Meeting of the Chieftains*

Remember scene in English history, "Field of the Cloth of Gold." Here, too, meeting of kings and chiefs in the King's Dale. Name them.

Picture Abram with his band, followed by the Canaanite chiefs and their men, all tired, but glad with victory. Then the rescued prisoners, and cattle, and wealth of many kinds. Note one prisoner especially. Then the King of Sodom, as he sees their spears far off flashing in the sunlight, comes out to meet and thank them; and then the strangest and most interesting figure of all, the white-haired chief coming down the mountain road, in priestly robes, and with a crown on his head. Who? Of what city? Meaning of its name? Meaning of his name? King of Righteousness. (See note on Melchizedek.) We know nothing further of him. Must have been a good and holy man, though a Canaanite. He was a priest of God, as well as a king, reigning in his peaceful city; and, curiously, his city seems to have escaped attack. Perhaps the invaders reverenced this holy king and priest; perhaps they feared that God would punish them if they injured him. Everybody seems to have reverenced him. King of Sodom made way for him. Abram bowed to receive his priestly blessing. Long centuries later his name appears in Psalms. In what connection? (Psalms cx.); and a thousand years later still an inspired Christian writer was so deeply impressed by him and his story that he writes of him as a type of our Lord's priesthood? Where is this? (Hebrews vii.) Will say more of him later on.

Now watch the meeting. King of Sodom, probably the new king (see xiv. 10), is approaching with his train; draws back respectfully when Melchizedek appears. They are all coming to do honour to one of the two Hebrews that had come years ago to Canaan as strangers. To which? Lot? Ah, no! Poor Lot, shrinking back in shame, perhaps mocked by Abram's men for the result of his choice. The hero of the day is God's true servant, who had tried to be faithful to God and the right. What does God say about "them that honour Me"? (1 Samuel ii. 30). First the royal priest gives his benediction in God's name. What does he call God? Then the King of Sodom makes a tempting offer in his gratitude. What? Thinks Abram should be glad to accept it. Is he? Why not accept it? (*v.* 23). Perhaps would not touch such wicked people's wealth; perhaps felt that God had promised to enrich him, and so would not let any man have to say that he had enriched him. At any rate, it shows that wealth is not a *very* important thing with the truest of God's servants.

§ 3. Melchizedek

Read Note on "Melchizedek," and teach whatever seems suitable for your class.

§ 4. Abram's Faith

Now the meeting of chieftains has broken up. Melchizedek is back at Salem, and Lot is gone into Sodom with the king and the remainder of the rescued men, and Aner and Eshcol and Mamre are away at their farms. And Abram is alone; the excitement of victory is over. Perhaps feeling dull and "flat" after it; perhaps a bit frightened. Why should he be? Had rescued prisoners from Chedorlaomer by God's help. But Chedorlaomer was great and powerful, and could come back and avenge himself on the lonely old chieftain. Lonely and old. There was the sting. No young chieftain growing up to take his place. No son, no daughter in his home. And yet God had promised that a great family and nation should spring from him. Can't you imagine his doubt, and perplexity, and sadness, as well as his fear of the invaders?

At this stage God's message comes. Perhaps in a vision, perhaps by a direct appearance to him. Count up for me all God's messages and appearances to him up to this. Now, tell me God's message. Was Abram content with it? What did he say? Yes, just now his heart so sore and lonely that even God's presence could not comfort him. "Lord, I am very lonely. Twenty-five years have I been wandering at Thy command. My poorest herdsmen and servants have children to love; I have nobody belonging to me. I have to take one of my servants for heir, and I am too old now to expect a son." Probably it may be called a want of faith, but is it not hard to blame him much? I don't think God blamed him much. "He knoweth our frame," etc. (Psalms ciii. 14). And I can fancy poor Abram in his depression schooling himself with difficulty to add, "But it is well, it must be right, since it is God's doing."

Now he is out beneath the midnight sky, and the

myriads of stars are gleaming above, and a deep awe is upon his spirit. In some mysterious way God is again beside him. Wonderful promise for an old man. What? Now question in detail about the sacrifice and the covenant. What is a covenant? What was God's covenant with Abram? Prophecy about Israelites in Egypt? For how long? One reason at least for not taking the land from the natives at once? (xv. 16). God always fair, and just, and patient. What other sign of His favour to the natives? Melchizedek and probably other priests to teach them. Abram was always taught this perfect fairness and righteousness of God. Even if it delayed Abram's happiness, yet he must always admire God's fairness. Once afterwards he showed this? (xviii. 25).

Now, tell me how Abram received all these extraordinary promises (*v.* 6). Twenty-five years before, at the call, he showed his faith. How? By *obeying*, in the face of all difficulties. Now showed his faith. How? *Believing*, in the face of all improbability. Just the same faith that produces both. If you have perfect faith in father as wise, and good, and anxious for your welfare, surely that faith will make you *obey* his will, for you know it must be a good will; and *believe* his word, for you know it must be a true word. Great joy to a father to see son unhesitatingly *believe* him in spite of all improbability, and unhesitatingly *obey* him in spite of suffering to himself, without even knowing the reason of the command. "My father could not be false, my mother could not do wrong." Ah! it is a glad day for a parent to hear that. Was God glad? (*v.* 6; *ch.* xxii. 16, 17).

Long afterwards St. Paul (Romans iv. 18-22) makes

this statement the centre of his teaching about faith. Justification by Faith is a doctrine often perverted, often babbled as an empty formula. "Only believe," "only believe," as if obeying were less important than believing. Look here at its true meaning. Abram believed God. Hebrew says, *"rested himself upon God."* It is a grand teaching for poor trembling strugglers. When a difficult, painful obedience is required, where is the strength like this resting upon God? When the terrors of conscience drive one to despair, where is the hope like this restful faith, that God loves you, and means the very best for you; that Christ, who died for us, meant it when He said, "Him that cometh unto Me," etc. That is the faith to make life strong, and brave, and peaceful.

NOTE ON MELCHIZEDEK

This story of Melchizedek has taken a strong hold on thinking religious people. His first appearance is so startling and mysterious—a priest of God amongst the dark Canaanite tribes—a priest, who is also a king—a priest, who brings forth bread and wine, the elements afterwards consecrated to sacred use by Christ—a priest whose official titles are King of Righteousness and King of Peace—a priest whose position was so commanding and assured that even Abram, "the father of the faithful," while refusing any deference to the King of Sodom, bowed down to receive his blessing, and willingly paid him tithes of the spoil which he had taken—a priest-king of whom we know nothing before or after; who flashes out, as it were, a meteor out of the past eternity, and then disappears for ever from our view—all this, even taken alone, would explain a good deal of the interest which has been roused in imaginative and religious minds by this ancient priest of Salem.

But there is more. A thousand years later an inspired writer (Psalms cx.), prophesying of the Messiah, goes back to the ancient story, and makes Melchizedek a type of the coming Son of David.

And, again, most striking of all, in another thousand years another inspired writer takes hold of this Psalm, and works out from it and from the Genesis story a theory about the eternal priesthood of Christ, and the abolition of the Levitical priesthood (Hebrews vii.). It is this last mysterious discussion that has, above all else, fastened attention on Melchizedek.

In early ages thoughts of awe and wonder were associated with his name. Some said he was the patriarch Shem, still living, though very old—some said he was an angel—some that he was the Holy Ghost—some that he was the Son of God appearing on earth in an earlier manifestation. But scholars of later days, after long and elaborate study, have come to the conclusion that he was but a simple human being—a priest and king of the Canaanite race—a remnant of the true religion from earlier days—probably a man of commanding character and deep holiness of life, owing his position solely to his character and to his official dignity as a priest of God.

There is no space here for a dissertation on the Melchizedek priesthood in Epistle to Hebrews. We need only point out that there is no good reason to think that the writer meant to speak of him as some supernatural being. Briefly, we may say that the writer, in teaching the doctrine of the priesthood of Christ, lays hold of the Melchizedek priesthood merely as a symbol or parable—(1) to symbolize the everlasting duration of Christ's priestly office; (2) to show that He might be a priest without possessing the legal qualifications for the Levitical priesthood. In the Levitical priesthood parentage and genealogy were of supreme importance. Christ's is an eternal priesthood, not dependent on such things. The symbolism of Melchizedek's priesthood catches hold of writer at once. History says nothing of his parentage or genealogy. This does not mean that he had not parentage and genealogy, but that history does not mention them. As far as history is concerned he is "fatherless, motherless, without genealogy." There is no mention of a beginning or ending. He flashes out of the past eternity for a moment, and then disappears from view, "having neither beginning of days nor end of life;" and in this respect, "made like unto the Son of God," who also flashed out of eternity for a moment into human ken, and then disappeared from view. Then the titles of the old priest-king catch on to his fancy—"King of Righteousness" and also "King of Peace." And he delights to trace in him more and more a type of the priesthood of our Lord.

The whole subject is worth careful study in a good commentary. We must content ourselves here with just giving this hint to the reader of the meaning of the mysterious treatise in the Epistle to the Hebrews.

There is another most interesting thought suggested

by this story. Abram and Melchizedek meet. Men of different race—men worshipping God by different names. Melchizedek called himself, not a priest of Jehovah, but a priest of El Elion. Two bigots might have quarrelled and cursed each other by their rival deities; but the deep inner essence of religion in each man made them recognize each other as brothers. Both were following after Righteousness and Peace; both were worshipping the all-holy God, possessor of heaven and earth, though under different names; and it seems a beautiful touch to express Abram's sympathy with Melchizedek, that in *v.* 22 he combines the two names, "I have lift up my hands to Jehovah El Elion." Thus do good men everywhere find their spiritual affinity. Underneath all differences in Christendom there is an underlying essence of religion, which is the same in all. In our own hymn book there are hymns by men of many religious denominations; and no one in reading them could distinguish the one from the other. God help us all to look for the best in men who differ from us, and, instead of emphasizing differences, to emphasize what we have in common, and thus draw nearer to God and to each other.

Notice, too, for advanced classes, the teaching here given that God was helping other races outside Israel, though Israel was specially helped and trained for sake of blessing others. Many such hints in Scripture. We have Melchizedek in Canaan, Balaam in Pethor, Job in Arabia, Jonah in Nineveh, etc.—men outside the chosen race worshipping God, and teaching about Him. By-and-by we shall have to learn of God's severe punishment on Canaan when their iniquity was full. Therefore emphasize here for them that Canaan was not yet rejected. Here was a priest of God, perhaps the last; perhaps little attended to by the people; or, perhaps, one of several such priests trying to teach them righteousness.

QUESTIONS FOR LESSON VIII

What do you know of the battle of the four kings against five?

What had Abram to do with it?

What do you know of (1) Melchizedek, (2) Chedor-laomer, (3) Aner, Eshcol and Mamre?

Abram's faith was shown (1) by obeying a difficult command, (2) by believing an unlikely promise? Explain.

THE COVENANT
AND ITS SIGN

Ch. XVI. 15 to end, and XVII.

§ 1. Birth of Ishmael

Last Lesson about God's repeated promise to the lonely Abraham. What promise? How long waited for? Strange fact in opening of story to-day—son born—whose? Was he the child promised by God? I think Abram and Sarai must have lost faith; got tired of waiting; or, perhaps, they thought they could bring about God's promise another way. So they decided that Abram should take another—a sort of inferior—wife, an Egyptian slave girl. Name? It was not right. It would be very wicked in our day, when we know God's will better. God judged men more gently in those early days of ignorance, and so did not blame them much; but all the same it was wrong. Abram and Sarai should have waited God's time. Yet it looked so improbable that I think they were puzzled. The Bible does not plainly condemn them. But you will see in later Lesson how much sorrow and

107

jealousy and bitterness it brought—quite spoiled the old happiness of the home. Whenever in doubt about God's will, the one safe thing is to do only the highest and best. Never stoop to lower action to bring about good. (Illustrate from children's lives.)

§ 2. God's Covenant Renewed

Now begin *ch.* xvii. Calculate how old Ishmael now? I think Abram now almost believed that this must be the promised son. Not for many years had he heard anything further, and one can fancy the old man getting deeply attached to the child—probably a strong, daring, attractive boy, rushing about with a boy's spear and bow and arrows, getting into all sorts of dangers, and not caring—such a boy as the whole camp would gladly accept as their young chieftain.

Yet things not quite satisfactory. Hagar proud and delighted, Sarah vexed and jealous; the home not as happy nor as holy as in the old, lonely days, when Abraham and Sarah clung closer to each other, and rested more in God. Even good people are in danger of drifting away into a less perfect life, if they do not watch. But God is very good to us in not being content to let us drift. So here.

Suddenly, after all these years, a Divine appearance again. Abram's attitude? (*v.* 3). Learn deep awe and reverence in God's presence. Not jesting or careless in church, or at your prayers. God's first words? Yes. Be perfect, true-hearted again. Don't be satisfied with lower life. Get nearer to God, as in olden days. Did he? Yes; we shall read in *ch.* xxii. how high he rose after this. No man ever rose higher. Are any of you drifting from God? Forgetting your prayers? Getting easily cross and selfish? Neglecting lessons or other duties? Getting satisfied with lower, careless life? Take this first verse to-night and pray about it, and God will lift you up like Abram; will help you to live the high happy life, that in the midst of lessons and play and work you may be always able to let your thoughts dart out for a moment towards God, and think, "I am His child. He is helping me upward."

Now, tell me in full about God's Covenant up to *v.* 8. Was covenant to Abraham only? (*v.* 7). I will be a God to thee, and to thy seed after thee. A good thing to be in the group who should share in this covenant. Tell me about change of name and meaning. Anything yet to make him think Ishmael not the heir of promise? But go on to *vv.* 15, 16. Something now that must have startled Abraham? How do you know? (*v.* 17). What does he say about Ishmael? Either he meant, "O Lord, let Ishmael do for your purpose; don't send me off waiting and hoping for years again;" or, "O Lord, don't forget poor Ishmael, whom I love; bless him also." At any rate it shows how he loved the boy. What answer to his prayer for Ishmael? How soon was Isaac to be born? So you see God's promise was to come true at last, though it seemed hopeless. God does not hurry; but God does not forget.

§ 3. *Little Children in the Old Covenant*

See beginning of Lesson VI. God wanted a religious family to grow into a religious nation, to keep up the knowledge of God in the world. So chose Abram. What was God on His side going to do for that religious family and nation that should spring from Abram? (*vv.* 7 and 8). But they were all to realize what God wanted them for; so everyone who was to share in the covenant had to go through a certain ceremony—circumcision—which corresponds to our baptism. What good in circumcision or baptism? One use clearly is this: They are like the coin that enlists a soldier. God did not want in His covenant a set of unthinking people born of Abram. No; each must go through a solemn ceremony of enlisting in God's army, to make him think seriously, to remind him what God wanted him for, and why He brought him into His covenant.

Tell me all the grown-up men who first enlisted? (*vv.* 24-27). Thus these men came forward to say, "I am God's soldier from this day, to help on righteousness, and I am in God's covenant, to be blessed and helped by Him. He will be a God unto me (*v.* 7), and I shall be His servant for ever."

But what about the little children, who could not promise, or understand, or act for God? Must they be shut out till they were grown up? Would God not be a God unto them till they could take on their promise? "Nay," he said, "I'll take all your little children in too, and all my side of the covenant of blessing shall come to them, though they can't do or promise anything. I'll trust them to do it when grown up. Meantime I'll grant them every blessing of the covenant. I will be their God as well as yours." So the Jewish Church received babies in circumcision and the Christian Church receives babies in Baptism, so taking them into God's covenant.

QUESTIONS FOR LESSON IX

Who were Ishmael's father and mother?

Was this what God intended?

God's further promise answers this question?

What was God's "covenant" with Abraham?

What is a covenant?

How did Abraham bring his people into it?

What of the children?

LESSON X

"SHALL NOT THE JUDGE OF ALL THE EARTH DO RIGHT?"

Genesis XVIII.

§ 1. Abraham and His Guests

Picture in your minds:—An Arab encampment in the hot, drowsy noonday ("in the heat of the day"); the cattle standing in the streams for coolness; the shepherds lying under the trees; the old chieftain, listless and languid, seated in the tent-door to get whatever breath of air may be moving, musing, perhaps, about this long-promised son, or about this wild, attractive young Ishmael, whom he is growing fond of. Suddenly he is startled to intensest wakefulness. Three men are standing right opposite! Something mysterious in their sudden appearance. They are evidently beings from the other world. Did he recognize their rank, or was it but the ordinary courtesy of an Arab chief? (See Hebrews xiii. 2, "unawares;" yet, on the other hand, see *v.* 3, the great reverence to central person in group.) At any rate, he *ran* to meet them, and—tell me all his hospitable

112

preparations (*v.* 3). See Abraham himself waiting on them. Notice "under the tree," the usual Arab and Indian place for guests to this day. In the unchanging East you might see the whole scene re-enacted to-day when strangers arrive at an encampment.

God loves hospitality. It is taught in Old Testament— taught by our Lord, and taught all through the Epistles (give some instances). Does hospitality mean only what people often do now, inviting their *rich* friends? That too, is good and friendly; but see Christ's direction (Luke xiv. 12). It is Christ's work. "Inasmuch as," etc. (Matthew xxv. 40). German story of little boy who left door open for the Lord to enter and sit with him and mother at their supper. A poor beggar looked in: "Oh, mother, perhaps the Lord could not come Himself, and sent this poor man instead!"

§ 2. Who Were the Guests?

Who were the three visitors? (See *v.* 1). Again see *v.* 10, "I will certainly," etc. Now see *v.* 16. Abraham walked with the three men (*v.* 22); *the men* went toward Sodom, and Abraham stood yet before THE LORD.

Now listen to the conversation "under the tree." Startling question asked. What? (*v.* 9). Surely Abraham must wonder and begin to suspect the rank of his Visitor. What did He promise? Who overheard? Did she believe it? How do you know? Did she laugh *aloud?* (*v.* 12). But God knows and hears everything. And Sarah was frightened at this mysterious knowledge (*v.* 15). Perhaps this, and the promise repeated, and the rebuke, affected

her, for her faith seems to have grown much stronger
(see Hebrews, xi. 11). Always remember the rebuke to
Sarah—"Is anything too hard for the Lord?"—when you
want to be really good and noble in your life, and think
it too much to hope for; or when you are praying for
some careless or wicked person whom you love. Only
be in earnest in seeking and striving, for "with God all
things are possible."

§ 3. "The Cry of the City"

Now concentrate our attention on Abram's prayer
for Sodom. Abram had walked with his visitors, and
now (v. 22) what happened? The great King of all the
worlds dismissed His servants to their work; and Abram,
in awe and solemn wonder, stood reverently before the
Lord.

And the Lord waits for him to muster courage to
speak, for He knows that Abram's heart is full of great
thoughts, and desires, and perplexities. What had the
Lord revealed to him on the way? What said about the
cry of Sodom? Did Abram hear any cry? No, but God,
who heard Sarah laugh, hears in every evil place the
cry of the oppressed and wronged; the cry of evildoers
rejoicing in their success; the sounds which are too
stifled for human ears, but which enter into the ears
of the Lord God of Sabaoth (see Genesis iv. 10). God
is always "going down to see" (v. 21); always close
about us—in our streets and schools, in our bedrooms;
everywhere, when we think no one is near. He is glad
if we are doing good, and "if not, I will know," He says.

And though God longs to bless us all, yet men and women, and boys and girls, must always remember that God will know, and that sin cannot escape punishment. And cities and Churches must remember that God is always "going down to see" what they are doing to keep life pure and holy, to promote righteous commercial life, and to see whether the slums, and the paupers, and the outcasts, and the aged, and sick poor, and the neglected little children, are being thought about by His people. There is a beautiful poem of Lowell's beginning:—

> "Said Christ the Lord, I go down to see
> How the men, My brethren, believe in Me."

It tells of the pomp with which He was received; of the worship and stately services, etc.; and how, in the midst of it all, He saw the poor people neglected, and the tempted people unhelped; and the groans of the sorrowful and oppressed rose up into His ears, and in scathing rebuke He turned on the people who were so pleased with themselves and their stately worship. God is always looking on the cities. God was visiting Sodom now in sternness and justice, for the cry of its awful vileness had risen into His ears.

§ 4. Abraham's Intercession

Did Abraham care whether the people of Sodom were punished? Yes. His great, generous heart took an interest in the people whom he had helped before. When? He cares for Lot; but he never mentions him. He evidently had more than Lot in view. They were bad people, yet he pleads for them, just as he had fought for them, earnestly, boldly, generously, unselfishly.

Think about this prayer. First see its fault; the bargaining and beating down of God's terms, as if God were less willing to be merciful than himself. He thought God not willing to save them if only forty-five good men there. Yet, what did he find at last? (*v.* 32). More anxious to save than was Abraham himself. Always so. We often pray doubtingly as if God were less kind and generous than ourselves; and all the time it is He who has prompted our prayer, and is more willing to hear than we are to pray.

How *earnest and persevering* the prayer was! All alone with God, perhaps for hours, he pleaded with his whole soul in his prayer. Oh! if we prayed for people like Abraham, or like Epaphras (Colossians iv. 12), "labouring fervently for you." I think we must lose a great deal for ourselves and others, because we are not enough in earnest. We are like the little boys that give a runaway knock at the door. We knock, and do not even wait, or hardly expect, the answer.

Again, Abraham prayed for people that he had done his best for before. He knew them, had fought for them, probably had tried to help them to be good. It seems a mockery to pray for anyone whose good we seek in no other way. We should be able to say: Lord, I have done, and am doing, what I can for him. Then the prayer will be real and acceptable unto God.

§ 5. The Third Exhibition of Abraham's Faith

Especially see the great *faith in the character of God.* Faith always means that. Faith in a character—refusal to believe anything but good of the person who is trusted, Abraham thought that there were some righteous amongst the heathen in Sodom; and it seemed to him unfair that all should be destroyed together. And he knew that God had the same sort of feelings as himself about what was fair or unfair. God had given him his conscience stamped with the Divine nature. It shrank from everything opposed to that nature. And Abraham looked up from his poor conscience up to the great, holy God above him, who had given him that conscience; and he knew that in Him was enthroned a moral nature infinitely grander and nobler than his own, and yet of the same kind. So he felt perfectly certain that God could do no wrong, and fearlessly he looks up into the face of his Divine Friend: "Shall not the Judge of all the earth do right?"

You remember the other exhibitions of his faith:— 1st, In obedience; 2nd, In believing God's promise; and now, the 3rd, The deep trust in the Divine conscience implanted in him, and educated in him, by God. This conscience is the dwelling-place of the Holy Spirit in us. It is God's great instrument for guiding our lives. This conscience told Abraham that injustice would be wicked in himself, and that it would be impossible in God; and he was certain that it was so. Nothing could shake his faith in it. God, who gave that guide to right, must always do right Himself. Remember always that faith in God means, at bottom, trust in a Person; trust in a character; trust in an infinite justice, and generosity, and holiness, and love; trust in a Being to whom it would be absolutely impossible that He should do anything ungenerous, or unfair, or unkind to any man.

That was Abraham's faith. That is the faith that will make our religion bright and happy, and make us willing, with glad heart, to trust and obey our Lord.

QUESTIONS FOR LESSON X

Who were the three visitors?

Tell me about Sarah's laughter?

Where does the question come in "Is anything too hard for the Lord?"

Tell fully of Abraham's pleading for Sodom.

Show the faith in it and also some want of faith?

ISHMAEL CAST OUT AND FOUND

Genesis XXI.

§ 1. The Birth of Isaac

Lesson after Lesson we have been thinking of the one great hope and craving in Abraham's life—something that God had promised him long, long ago. What? Wearily he waited year after year, trying to keep his faith. Then he and Sarah, when it seemed hopeless to wait longer, seem to have thought that God's promise might mean something different; and so the girl Hagar was brought as a secondary or inferior wife, and the child Ishmael was born, and Abraham grew fond of him; and I dare say he sometimes thought that this was the way in which God's promise would be fulfilled (*ch.* xvi. 16-18). Was it? No. What did God tell him after Ishmael's birth? (*ch.* xviii. 16). So he was thrown back again on God's promise, and had to wait on patiently still.

Now at last comes the fulfilment. After how many

119

years? It was a great miracle that a child should be born to such very old people. Nobody ever heard of the like before. I think God meant them to see that it was a miraculous thing, and to feel great awe and solemnity about the purposes for which He had called them and planned their lives. Were they glad? What did Sarah say? Explain Sarah's remark in *v.* 6. Isaac—the name given by God before the child's birth—means "Laughter," and her words were a play on the name. We may be sure there was great rejoicing at Isaac's birth; and surely great reverence and solemnity, too, at the thought of God's promise coming true after twenty-five years waiting.

§ 2. Isaac and Ishmael

At *v.* 8 a new part of the story. Probably about two years had passed, as was usual in the East; and at the weaning, as to-day in India, a great festival was made by Abraham. Oxen and fatlings were killed, and feasting went on in the tents, and the servants had a holiday, and there was laughter and rejoicing through the encampment. But there was one instance of laughter that was not pleasant? Yes. As the mistress of the encampment moved about receiving congratulations, suddenly she came on the big boy Ishmael, mocking and jeering. You know the sort of clumsy jokes that a boy of fourteen loves to make. One cannot wonder that Hagar was angry and disappointed. Her position and that of her son were quite overthrown by the birth of the young heir. And in her bitterness she had evidently stirred up Ishmael to mock at the baby, and to jeer at his "old mother."

Was Sarah very angry? How do you know? (*v.* 10). So angry she would not even call them by their names. "The son of this bondwoman." Twice she repeats the cruel name. The jealousy between these two women was very bitter and long-standing. Fifteen years before it had sprung up when Hagar, taken in as Abram's secondary wife, had become impertinent and insulting to the chieftainess of the tribe; and so fiercely did Sarah resent it then that Hagar had to fly from the place (*ch.* xvi). God's will is that a man should have but one wife, and wherever this law is broken, misery must come. So here. Probably Sarah suffering now for her own suggestion that Abraham should take Hagar for his wife, instead of waiting patiently for God's promises. At any rate, Sarah's feeling is little changed from what it was fifteen years before. Out must go this bondwoman and her son!

§ 3. Cast Out

Of course the complaint was brought to Abraham. How did he feel about it? Yes. Fond of the boy, and probably of Hagar, too; and shrinking from turning them out on the world.

But Sarah would give him no peace. Perhaps, besides her jealousy of Hagar, she had a woman's keen perception that it was best for Abraham to be left entirely dependent on this child of promise.

All day he brooded over it. What should he do? Last time that Sarah advised him (to take Hagar to wife), he had been unwise in doing it. What should he do now? How did he find out? (*v.* 12). I think he

121

fell asleep when tired of thinking over it, and God, in a dream, gave him direction and encouragement too. What direction? (*v.* 12). What encouragement? (*v.* 13). Did God's direction mean that He approved of Sarah's spirit? No. Of course, we are only guessing that it was mainly jealousy that moved Sarah. If we are right, we must only say that God, too, saw it was wise to send away Hagar and Ishmael, even though He disapproved of the spirit which prompted it. It was very hard on Abraham to part with the boy whom he had so grown to love. But God promised to take care of Ishmael and make him head of a nation (*v.* 13).

So in the early morning, kindly and tenderly, he sent them away. He himself tended them—did not leave it to servants to do it. It may look heartless to a careless reader; but I think the student of Abraham's life will feel that he sent them away with sorrow and that, after providing them with food and water, and probably the trinkets that could be used as money, he trusted them to his God to take care of them for the future. We must judge this act by what we know of his whole life.

§ 4. *Found*

Was he right in thus trusting? Tell me what happened? Poor Hagar! what a fearful experience to see her boy dying of the most horrible death—death by thirst. How angry she would feel against Sarah, against Abraham, perhaps against God. "Much God cares for poor me so long as his favourite Abraham is all right and happy!"

People often treat God thus when things go wrong with them. God has to bear a good deal of that. Are they right? Was Hagar right? All the time that she was thinking evil of Him, God had been watching over her like a father over his child. We are not told that she even prayed to Him, though she must have learned to pray in Abraham's home. But in the midst of her agony and sudden rebellion came the kind voice, "What aileth thee, Hagar?" And immediately she remembered a similar scene fifteen years before (*ch.* xvi), when God had cared for her, a helpless outcast; and the conviction comes to her that God is still watching over her and her boy. Tell me the rest. And as God was caring for Ishmael all along, he, too, should become a great nation. But he can grow and develop best in the wild, free desert. He, too, can accomplish part of God's great plan.

Thus the lesson comes to us that, while God specially elects certain men for the high places in His great world-plan, He is kind and loving to *all*. He has blessing and help for those whom He does not appoint as leaders; they, too, are to have their own smaller influence in the history of the world. Ishmael must not take Isaac's place—"In Isaac shall thy seed be called"—but Ishmael has his own place, and God will help and bless him too. He will help and bless everyone who will let Him do so. He cares about everyone on the face of the earth, though He does not elect all to special positions. Read note on Election after Lesson XIV.

QUESTIONS FOR LESSON XI

In the rejoicings about Isaac's birth something vexed Sarah?

What was the result of this?

Was God forgetting young Ishmael and his mother?

How do you know?

What is the lesson of this?

THE SACRIFICE OF ISAAC

Genesis XXII. to v. 20, and XXIII. 17 to end

§ 1. Abraham's Faith

Recapitulate last Lesson. Birth of Isaac, joy of parents, etc.

About fifteen years have elapsed since the baby boy came. He was now a strong lad. Now a strange scene. Dim morning twilight. Sarah is asleep. Isaac is asleep. Farm-servants not yet stirring. But Abraham is moving about already, pale and haggard with an awful trouble that has come to him in the visions of the night—a secret trouble, rending his very soul, but which he dare not tell to his wife or child. What was it? Yes. "God did tempt (i.e., test or prove) Abraham." (*v.* 1). Satan *tempts* to produce evil; God *tests* to bring out the good. And every great crisis, every hard decision about duty has this double side. In every temptation God is testing, Satan is tempting.[1] Did God really mean him to kill

---

[1]Compare 2 Samuel xxiv. 1, with I Chronicles xxi. 1. The very temptation which in one book is ascribed to God, is in

125

his son? No. Perhaps he misunderstood. Perhaps he thought God was recalling His gift; that He had found him unworthy of it. It is the noblest hearts that are quickest to think that; it is the purest hearts that are quickest to feel self-reproach. But, at any rate, *Abraham believed that it was meant* that he should slay him; and God let him believe it in order to test him, and to make him win, by that supreme hour of trial, the grandest faith which the world has ever seen in man.

Would not Abraham be horrified at the thought, and think it wrong? No. Sacrifice of children was common amongst the heathen, and Abraham did not know all that even a Sunday-school child knows to-day about God's will. But poor Abraham tried his best, at terrible cost, to do the little that he knew. Tell me any cases of, or references to, child-sacrifice? (Judges xi. 31; Micah vi. 7; 2 Kings xvi. 3). Perhaps Abraham had seen such, and wondered "should I be capable of such a sacrifice for Jehovah as these people do for their gods? Do I care enough for Him to sacrifice myself, or, harder still, my boy? Am I only offering cheap sacrifices of lambs, and withholding from Him what would be a fearful pain to give?" To a very noble heart like his that thought would

---

the other book ascribed to the devil. And it is very possible, says a writer in *The Expositor*, that if we had two inspired biographies of Abraham, both written by ancient Hebrew scribes, one of them would say, "God tempted Abraham," and the other, "Satan tempted Abraham;" while if we were so fortunate as to have *three* biographies instead of two, in all probability the third would contain a sentence which would reconcile both statements—such a sentence as we have in the story of a still greater temptation: "Then was Jesus led up *of the Spirit* into the wilderness to be tempted *of the devil.*"

come with crushing force; and so when the conviction came to him that God demanded this supremest pain, he did not think it wrong, only awfully difficult.

Can't you imagine the old man that morning in his agony, hiding it from Sarah and from the boy, trying to nerve himself to the awful duty, thinking to himself, "If it be God's will, surely I can trust Him. If it be wrong to slay the boy, surely He will hinder me. But if it be right, if it be really His will, I will do it! Yes! I will do it, even if it should break my heart. My boy will still be in God's hands Who gave him. He can even raise him from the dead (Hebrews xi. 12) if He thinks it best. At any rate, I have trusted Him all my life, and I will trust Him even through this." Wonderful faith! How had he learned it? Did such faith come all at once? No; by slow degrees, step by step, since the day he left Haran, God had been "testing Abraham," as He is testing us all, and thus training us. All the hard things, the painful duties, and worries, and vexations, are God's gradual testing and training. And Abraham had been trying to respond. How? What is the real test of faith and love to God? Is it our talkings, or our feelings? No. The true test is how much are we prepared *to do and suffer for God and right.* "He that hath my commandments, and *keepeth* them, he it is that loveth Me." (St. John xiv. 21).

Did Abraham delay? (*v.* 1). "Early in the morning." That promptness is the great safeguard. When you see a duty, go at it at *once.* Don't wait to reason, or persuade yourself out of it. Probably before any of the farm-servants were stirring, the old man was away with the boy and the wood, and the terrible secret that was torturing his heart. Now, think of the father and son, day after day, northward, ever northward, to the land of Moriah; think of the father's heart torn with anguish, as he watched Isaac amusing himself with the changing scenes and events of the journey. Now the attendants are left.[1] Then watch them both—the two solitary figures up the mountain path, the man carrying the fire and the knife, the boy bending lightly under the load of the wood. "They went both of them together." At last Isaac wonderingly breaks the silence, asking—what? Abraham's reply? Comment in Hebrews? (*ch.* xi. 19). Perhaps some dim hope that God would raise him up; at any rate, God *could*, and so he left it. There is nothing grander than the thought: I know God can deliver me. I trust He will; but IF NOT, IF NOT, even still I will not flinch. Compare three young men in fiery furnace: We believe our God *will* deliver us; but if not, if not, still we will not serve thy gods, nor be disloyal to the right within us. Now, at last, the awful moment comes when he must tell Isaac. Slowly, lingeringly, he piles stones for the altar, slowly lays out the wood, and now—a pause of agony. He looks into the boy's wondering face, and, with a mighty force upon himself, tells him all.

Inspiration draws a veil over that last tender, awful scene—the sobbing good-bye—which told how much mortal man could do for love of God.

---

[1]The Jerusalem Targum says they were Ishmael and Eliezer of Damascus.

§ 2. Isaac's Faith

But what of Isaac—is no honour due to him? How old do you think he was? Could carry the load of wood up the mountain; must have been a big boy, able to resist if he chose. Did he? No. It seems that the wonder and grandeur of his father's faith and self-surrender touched him.

There is a contagion in all nobleness; and, like Jephthah's daughter, only not so ignorantly, he, too, bowed himself to what seemed the will of God. He knew he was sent to earth for God's great purposes, not for his own. God knew best, and so he carried up the wood of the sacrifice like Christ carrying the Cross, and laid himself down, like Christ, to die. Think of the joy of God seeing such a sight—the grand, heroic obedience of the father, the simple, loyal submission of the son—for what they believed to be the will of God. Hard, and puzzling, and awful though it seemed, they believed God's will was a good will, though they could not see it to be so. They felt that seeing was not their business. They must just go straight on doing as they were told, without ever thinking what the result would be. So we. Every morning let life of the day begin with the question, What would God have me to do? In all the acts of the day keep repeating it. In the prayer and self-examinations at night inquire, Have I been asking in all my decisions what would God wish done, and not caring for any consequences?

Now tell me the ending of the story. Yes. How soon did God interfere? Not till the sacrifice of Abraham's and Isaac's will was complete; the last sobbing good-byes said; the knife raised for the awful stroke. Why not interfere earlier, and save them much of the agony? It would not have been the same testing, nor wrought in their characters the same good.

What did God feel about it all? (*vv.* 16, 17). Oh! think of it. How God gloried in that man's loyalty and strength of character. How it thrilled the Almighty to the depth of His Being. "By myself have I sworn, saith the Lord, for because thou hast done this thing, and hast not withheld thy son, thine only son: that in blessing I will," etc.

§ 3. Lessons for Us

LESSON I.—If we desire that God should accomplish in us the very highest best He intends for us, the way to attain it is—what? To aim always at doing what we think to be His will, in spite of all unpleasantness, and pain, and trouble. Make the rule of life never to do or decide anything without asking, What would the Lord Jesus have me to do? Every morning begin the day with this thought. All day ask this question, and at night examine yourself by means of it.

LESSON II.—What use is this story to us? Of course it shows how the religion of Jehovah forbade offering human sacrifices so common amongst the heathen of that time. But it shows something more important than this. Shows how God delights in the nobleness of self-sacrifice (*v.* 16). That is the very essence of God's own character. God delighted in Abraham's act because it was just what He would do Himself—what He did do. When? For whose sake? Yes. That was the greatest lesson ever taught about the character of God. From Mount Moriah, where a father gave his son, and received God's deliverance, we look to Mount Calvary, where the Great Father gave His Son as a sacrifice, and there was no deliverance. God rouses us to the life of love and self-sacrifice by exhibiting His own self-sacrifice. *God is Love,* i.e. *God is Self-sacrifice.* To live for others, to give and sacrifice Himself for others, is God's eternal joy. He is always doing it from all eternity. He will always be doing it. To us poor strugglers after God it is still a pain, but yet a pain in some degree mixed with joy and admiration.[1] When we get to heaven, when we grow like Christ, we shall learn His lesson; that to give oneself for others, to sacrifice everything for others, is the highest joy possible in the universe—so great and pure a joy that it swallows up the pain.

But can anyone now follow Abraham's and Isaac's examples? What do you think of these cases?—(1) A dear old clergyman whose youngest and favourite son was asked to go out as an Indian missionary. Poor old man, I remember how it rent his very soul. He could hardly bear to part with his boy. He knew he could

---

[1]Mr. Ruskin points out how even the crowd instinctively admires and honours self-sacrifice:—"A soldier's trade, verily and essentially, is not slaying, but *being slain.* This, without well knowing its own meaning, the world honours him for. A bravo's trade is slaying, but the world has never honoured bravoes."

never live to see him again. But the brave, true heart yielded up its will for sake of God and the poor heathen. (2) A clever young lad in college, most ambitious to be a doctor. He was an only son. He knew it would be an intense pleasure to his father if he would stay with him to manage the farm, and keep the old home bright. He hated farming. He had set his heart on being a doctor. It was a hard struggle, fought out on his knees before God; and then the boy rose up, resigned and brave, gave up all that he had set his heart on; settled down to the dull, monotonous life in the country. (3) A young girl with a letter in her hand inviting her on the most delightful visit to her cousins in the country. Just what she longed for. As she raised her eyes, she saw the tired look on her poor mother's face. Instantly, without a word, she crumpled the letter into her pocket, and settled down for the hot summer months to lighten the work at home. Her mother never even knew of the invitation. But God knew and cared. And somehow, in every one of these cases, as soon as people yielded to God's will, and sacrificed themselves for others, as God does, then came God's peace—the peace that passeth all understanding.

> "O God! that I might spend myself for others:
>   May that grace come to me;
>   That I might pour my life into my brother's—
>   A sacrifice to Thee."

QUESTIONS FOR LESSON XII

Meaning of "God did tempt Abraham"?

Why did Abraham think of sacrificing his son?

How far was he right and how far was he wrong?

What was there in his surroundings that might make him think it right?

Does Isaac deserve any credit in this matter?

How was Isaac saved?

Repeat the words which show how pleased God was.

Show how similar self-sacrifice is possible in our day.

How has God shown self-sacrifice for us?

THE WOOING OF REBEKAH

Genesis XXIV. to v. 29, and v. 58 to end

This lesson is more naturally fitted for a girls' class. I have written it with such in view. But it can be taught in any class.

§ 1. Eliezer's Commission

Remember last Lesson, when Isaac as a big boy went up Mount Moriah to die. Twenty-five years have passed before we come to this chapter—ordinary, uneventful for the most part, but with one awful year amongst them, when, in her husband's absence, Sarah died on the heights of Kirjath-arba, and Abraham came back broken-hearted to the encampment to mourn and to weep for her.

What a lonely place it was now for him! No one to sympathize, as she would have done, in his trouble, and his hopes, and his faith in God; no one to talk to about the old home in Ur, which they two had left together fifty years ago. So the two lonely men mourned together for her; for Isaac seems to have loved his mother with a great, strong love, and to have mourned with an intense sorrow (see *ch.* xxiv. 67).

Now (*v.* 2) we have Abraham and his old steward closeted together. What about? Yes; they want her all the more, because they are so lonely. Why not get a wife in Canaan? Must have been very nice Hittite and Canaanite girls, perhaps daughters of Abraham's friends, Aner, Eshcol, and Mamre (xiv. 13), and others? Probably they were chiefly godless people in Canaan, though not as bad as later (see Deuteronomy vii. 3). Besides, news from the old far-away home had come to Abraham (xxii. 20, etc.), and probably turned his heart to his own kindred. Old Eliezer saw a difficulty in the way. What? (*v.* 5). What did Abraham reply to him? (*v.* 6). Did Abraham think that his servant would fail? Why not? (*v.* 7). So we notice in him three things to be admired and imitated. What? Let the class try to guess—1st, he was not content to let his son marry a rich girl in Canaan, who could bring him flocks, and herds, and power. The son, who was the heir of the promises, must be married to a good woman, even if she were poor; 2nd, he committed the whole thing to God; 3rd, he believed that God would help him in it; "He shall send His angel before thee," etc. So Eliezer started off on his journey, encouraged by his master's faith.

§ 2. Eliezer's Prayer

The next scene is in far-off Mesopotamia. The old steward, with his train of camels and gifts, has been travelling wearily on for many days; and now, in the sunset light before him, he sees at last the little town of Haran, the city of Nahor, and the girls of the town out chatting and gossiping by the wells, as is usual in the evenings, and filling their pitchers for the morning use; and the sight of the girls reminds him how critical and delicate is his business.

"How can I, a dull old man, choose the sort of wife that my young master needs? Is it to be one of the maidens yonder at the wells? Who is she, and where is she, that shall be the young mistress in our encampment?" Don't you think he might well be puzzled and frightened at the task before him? What help did he seek? Ah! that is the true help in perplexities. Where had he learned to seek God? Yes; clearly Abraham tried to have a religious household about him. No man could live as close to God as he did without his household feeling the power of religion. How can religious men make their servants and children religious? Is it by talking about it? or scolding them about it? No; there is only one sure way—by being very religious and very *lovable* themselves. *Real* religion is the most lovable thing on earth, and makes the most lovable people. There are some religious people who wish to be religious, but, through their own fault, are somehow not lovable. They often hinder young people from being religious. A girl said to the writer lately: "I don't want to be religious, for some religious people that I know are very disagreeable!"

If you know any such, don't blame their religion for it; always remember that it is their own little peevishness, or pettishness, or want of sympathy, which remains in spite of their religion: though they have some religion, they have not enough to make them really unselfish and lovable. When they grow nearer to Christ, they will grow more lovable and nice to be with.

What was Eliezer's prayer? (*v.* 1). "Send me good speed this day." Suppose we all used it every morning, and especially on any critical day in our lives! Now tell me exactly what guidance Eliezer asked (*vv.* 13-15). Why? Would it be any sign of her character? Did God hear his prayer? How long had he to wait? (*v.* 15). Read promise, Isaiah lxv. 24. When God does not answer so quickly, there is probably some good reason. Amongst the girls laughing and chatting together on the way to the wells came one just at this moment, a very pretty girl (*v.* 16), and evidently a bright, lively, generous-hearted girl, too. Who was she? She was the chief's daughter; but in those simple days a "lady" did not think it degrading to work—a true lady never does. She could cook well (xxvii. 9), and mind cattle, and carry her pitcher of water as well as any girl in the village. There was evidently something winsome which attracted the old steward. A pretty face and winsome manner would naturally do that; but these are only surface things, and Eliezer is too wise to trust them. What is the most lasting and important of any girl's attractions? Yes. Religion. A noble, beautiful soul. Can't always discover that at once. What is first and most easily discovered attraction in a girl? Yes. Prettiness; and if a girl has that, it attracts us, and makes us look for the further attractions. What is the next most easily discovered? Quickness, brightness, pleasant disposition. And the last and most important and enduring of all? An earnest religious heart. With God the first of these attractions shall be last, and the last first. Can you explain? It is so with mankind, too. Explain. Yes; when the pretty face and the cleverness have lost their charm, right on to old age, the attraction of the beautiful soul remains. Learn by heart this: Kingsley's advice to girls—

> "Be good, sweet maid, and let who can be clever;
>   Do lovely things, not dream them, all day long;
>   And so make life, death, and that vast forever,
>   One grand, sweet song."

Eliezer, then, is not content with prettiness and brightness; so he tests her character. How? Yes; evidently she is kindly as well as pretty, and his heart warms towards her, as with delight he sees his whole test fulfilled. Wonderingly, as if it were too good to be true, he questions her. What? (*vv.* 23-26). And then? (*v.* 27). Yes. With glad heart he gives thanks to God. He seems to think that God did it all for Abraham's sake only. Do you? I think that that simple, lovable, unselfish old steward, seeking God's help for his master, not for himself, is the sort of man whom God would love to grant things to.

§ 3. *The Bride Coming Home*

Did Rebekah wait till he was done his thanksgiving? (*v.* 28). Just like a girl, she was off at once at a run to tell them at home: "Who do you think is coming? You told me about our rich cousins in Canaan! Well, their steward is outside. What do you think he has come for? Look at the ear-rings and bracelets he has given me." And then she told the whole story.

What was her brother's name? We read of him afterwards. He was covetous then. I am rather amused to see his covetousness even now. It is when he sees the ornaments, that he rushes out to invite the old man in. Then, can't you imagine what a night of talking they had, and how they sat up listening unwearied to the story of their kinsman's greatness, and the errand on which he had sent his steward; and how the girl, with bright, eager eyes and parted lips, sat listening to this wonderful romance that had suddenly come into her life; and how they started off in state next morning? and how Eliezer beguiled the weary way for her with descriptions of the new home, and stories about Isaac, especially that story of the day when the boy had gone up Moriah, and loyally offered his young life as a sacrifice to God? How a generous girl's heart would throb at such a tale, especially about her lover. What a strange, wonderful home she was going to, and how awfully real was God's presence there!

When and how did she meet her lover? What was he doing? Was it not a beautiful beginning for their new life together, that the first sight she got of her future husband was when he was at his evening meditations in the field? When you remember what Isaac was, and the holy household he had been brought up in, you will easily believe that they were holy meditations about

God, as well as, no doubt, about the young bride, too, that God was bringing into his life. Eliezer must have told her a great deal about him. She seemed to know him and love him already; and as she saw the young man crossing the fields to meet her, and the steward whispered, "It is my young master," she alighted down from the camel, and he turned straight from his thoughts of God to his thoughts of her; or, rather, he mingled thoughts of God and of her together—the most blessed attitude in which any man could meet his bride.

I'm afraid this life did not go on as it began. There must have been some fault, I fear, in the home to explain a story like that before us in next lesson. When we come to it, I shall ask your opinion.

QUESTIONS FOR LESSON XIII

Who was Eliezer of Damascus?

What were the two old men conferring about?

Show Abraham's faith here.

What was Eliezer's simple prayer?

What do you know about Rebekah?

Who was Laban?

How did Rebekah meet her future husband?

LESSON XIV

JACOB AND ESAU

Genesis XXV. 29 to end, and Ch. XXVII. to v. 41

This is a long and important Lesson. Only time for the most important parts. Don't waste a moment unnecessarily. Let class read *ch.* xxv. 29, etc., and examine. Teacher should read *ch.* xxvii.; it is too long for class to read, and they will spoil the pathos of it. For senior classes, perhaps, the main thought in Note on election may be used. At any rate teacher should study it.

§ 1. Isaac and Rebekah

What was last story about Isaac and Rebekah? What the previous one about Isaac? Their first meeting gave great hopes for their future lives. Were these hopes quite realized?

A great many years have elapsed. The young bride and her lover are now aged people. Is it not a disappointment now to find Isaac setting his heart so much on nice venison to eat (xxv. 28; xxvii. 4), and

141

Rebekah joining with Jacob to deceive the old blind man? Perhaps poor old Isaac was in his dotage, and sick. Men shut up in a room *do* get the habit of thinking much about their dinners. But he seems to have fallen back in his religion. The heroic boy who would lay down his life for God ought to have a grander old age. It is easy to spoil a life. Perhaps life had been too easy for him. Abraham had had all the struggle, and Isaac inherited the comforts. That often stunts a boy. To have to struggle and make his own way, and fight fierce temptations, is what will make a man of him.

Then see the favouritism. Each had a favourite. People often love opposites. Isaac, dreamy and quiet, loved the active, daring Esau. Rebekah, active and bustling, loved the boy who was, probably, the weaker and more dependent on her. Mothers usually do. Favouritism is bad. I think it made Isaac try to give the blessing to his favourite against God's will. It made Rebekah lie for her favourite.

§ 2. *Esau*

Now look at the two brothers. Utterly different. Which of the two brothers do you like best? And you? You? Of course, you are all up in arms for "poor wronged Esau." And you think that the teacher is bound to defend Jacob. And you feel that the Bible seems to do so. And you feel that it is not quite generous and fair.

But teachers and clergy, too, *when younger and less educated in Scripture*, always stood up for Esau. What puzzled them was that the Bible does not. That sets one thinking. Must be some reason for it. Must be that they had not read the story thoughtfully enough, nor quite understood the characters of the two brothers. For you know God is absolutely generous and fair; more so than you, and therefore He, too, would prefer Esau if he were the nobler man. Now let us think and examine.

First look at Esau. Make picture of him in your mind: strong, shaggy, red-haired hunter—full of vigour and power—every inch a man—hot, passionate, generous, impulsive, with a sort of Irishman's recklessness as to what may come to-morrow—a man who could be brave, who could forgive—could scatter gifts with lavish hand—the sort of man that men often like and seek as a comrade and leader. And yet, as we learn from the disapproval of him in the Bible, a man utterly worldly and sensual—would give up anything for a passing enjoyment. Excitement, pleasure, hunting, eating, drinking, were everything to him. No deep sense of God or of the future. No care for spiritual things. His good and evil acts alike spring from the impulse of the moment, not at all from principle or sense of duty. See him come in hungry (*ch.* xxv. 30). What did he see and smell? Yes; and he was such a big baby that he could not wait for an hour to make red pottage for himself. No! "Oh, give me that red pottage, and I'll do anything you ask." "Will you give me your birthright for it?" "Yes, anything, only let me have it! I'm at the point to die." Think of a big, strong man going on like that because he could not get his dinner in time. What would you say of a young man to-day who gave up his prospects thus? Jacob was mean, and tricky, and unbrotherly *at this period* of his life, before religion had purified him; but Esau, with all his courage and strength, was contemptible—a slave to his passions. Greedy, unbridled men like him are not fit to be fathers of great nations, or to help forward the world as God wanted. If our ancestors had all been like him, we should be ignorant, heathen savages to-day. God wants a higher type, to help Him to lift up the world.

Do you think there are people of the Esau type now? Boys strong, brave, merry, good-natured; girls, bright, pleasant, handsome, attractive, but without real religion. These attractions are God's good gifts, and grand gifts they are when accompanied with faithful hearts towards God, but very dangerous otherwise; for the attractive boys and girls and men and women become leaders of others, and if they don't care for spiritual things—i.e., for putting God, and right, and duty first of all—they do more harm than unattractive people, for comrades admire them, and are in sympathy with them, and so get low ideals of life, and think that pleasure is more important than right-doing.

§ 3. Jacob

But was not Jacob worse? Yes; it seems to me that while Esau came into the world with certain natural attractions, Jacob came into the world with none at all; and yet look what he rose to through religion and God's grace. *In his youth* he was a liar, a schemer—what schoolboys would call a sneak. He deceived his father, cheated his brother, made bargains even in his prayers with God. He made up for his want of courage and manliness by being unpleasantly sharp and clever.

As we look at the two brothers *in their youth*, no one could hesitate in preferring Esau. Yes; but *at the close of their lives* how would it be? Though one was a proud, successful Arab chieftain, the ancestor of a princely race, with his desires all gratified—plenty of eating, and drinking, and hunting, and wives, and children, and power; and the other was a poor broken old man, with his young wife long dead, and his favourite boy, as he thought, murdered; a poor, sorrowful old man, bowing down in deep humility before God, and crying from the depths of a contrite heart, "I am not worthy of the least of all Thy mercies."

What is the lesson of it all? That there is a deep difference—deep as eternity—between mere *natural attractiveness* and real *character*, formed by the grace of God through discipline and trial, and that God can, out of very poor material, make a holy saint. That is great encouragement for poor creatures like us, when we hate ourselves for our meanness and faults, and yet long to be good. Jacob was mean and tricky; but there was a something within him that would not let him rest in his meanness and trickiness. Perhaps the very knowledge of his meanness, etc., made him determined to cling to God. And he did; and he bore sorrow, and suffering, and pain, and trouble all his life, till God had burned the meanness and trickiness out of him, and made him a noble old man—Israel, the "Prince with God."

§ 4. The Birthright

What was the birthright? Was it merely to get his father's property? At any rate, Jacob did not get it. To be the heir of God's promise; to be associated with Abraham in God's covenant; to inherit Palestine; to be the ancestor of the chosen race, through which all the earth should be blessed; to have the blessing of his dying father, so highly prized to this day by the Eastern peoples—this was the grand future which Jacob's ambition sought.

Don't forget, then, what grand things Jacob was aiming at. He was a dishonest and untruthful Eastern shepherd. Had not been well brought up, I think, by his parents; was mean and selfish; but had something in him higher than Esau had, and which God could make something of. He pursued his ambition with a good deal of selfishness. Yet how much higher and better an ambition than Esau's, which was—what?—to get a good dinner, and without delay. I don't think Esau was capable of appreciating this birthright, even if he had got it. If it had been something to eat or drink, he would not have sold it so easily. Tell me now exactly the aim of each of the men, so as to compare them clearly.

Do people ever sell their birthrights now, like Esau? What is your birthright? To be "a member of Christ, the child of God, an inheritor of the Kingdom of Heaven." Think of it: to be a member of Christ's kingdom here, making life happy, and holy, and beautiful for others; to live as God's child on earth, and be received into His glorious kingdom above by-and-by. Was it as good as

Esau's? Better. Could you sell it away? Ah! many a one has done it for a miserable mess of red pottage—the drunkard for his mess of red wine, or the worldly man for his handful of red gold, etc., etc. Read Hebrews xii. 16. Pray to God to keep you from doing it.

§ 5. *Jacob's Deceit*

Question carefully on *ch.* xxvii. Indicate that God's purpose was to make Jacob the ancestor of the chosen people, and that God's purposes would be exactly and beautifully worked out if men would everywhere follow their highest ideals and most generous instincts; but that, in this evil world, God has to take account of evil-doing, and over-rule even that, to bring about good, *while punishing the evil-doer.* So here. Esau's greediness (*ch.* xxv.) and Jacob's treachery (*ch.* xxvii.) are all *punished, but not allowed to spoil God's plan.*

I can but indicate a few lines of thought here. The chapter is full of lessons. Point out the *gradual* growth of Jacob's sin. Important lesson. I don't think he was either bad enough or daring enough to plan such a sin if could have foreseen it all. He had qualms about the first step, but not strong-willed enough to say No, when it was only proposed to personate Esau. Hear his weak protest. Not "It is wrong, mother, and I can't do wrong for anyone." (That was the protest of his nobler son in Egypt). No; but "my father might find me out." Whenever a man takes that position, he is sure to fall. Step by step he went on. The first step of personating Esau started a train of further sins. Putting on the skins;

then the direct lie, "I am Esau;" then the blasphemous statement, "The Lord thy God brought it to me." Think of the shrinking as he felt forced on from step to step. Think of his terror when Isaac said, "Come near, that I may feel thee, my son." (Luther says: "If I had been Jacob then, I should have dropped the dish in terror, and run.")

That is the devil's plan always. Step by step. Such things happen every day—e.g., young man, not intending much evil, bet on horse race; then borrowed money to pay his losses, honestly intending to pay it; then, being pressed, took from employer's cash-box, intending to refund it; then discovery, lying, false swearing, prison, disgrace, ruin. Thus the devil urged him on step by step. Oh! take care of the beginning of sin.

Point out, too—referring to Hebrews xii. 17, that Esau found no room for repentance—the irrevocableness of our deeds. Not that he could not repent. He had repentance, and remorse, and sorrow. The tears show that; but the passage means he found no means to undo his act of selling the birthright, of which this was consequence. So with us—lost youth, lost purity, lost opportunity cannot be recalled. You might notice, too, that Esau had not so much right to feel wronged as he thought—Esau had deliberately bartered away that birthright, and with it, it would seem, the right to the blessing.

In spite of your teaching on *ch.* xxv., the pupil's sympathy will still be with Esau and against Jacob here. That is as it should be. Don't try to oppose it. Be intensely careful and apprehensive lest you should distort the fresh, healthy, moral consciousness of the children, and let them believe that Jacob was any the less wrong because God's purpose would be accomplished by his evil act. Don't let them think that God's sympathies would be opposed to theirs in this story. Surely God was angry at Jacob's treachery, though He made allowance for his circumstances, which we cannot; and surely God was very sorry for Esau, as for every sinner who has bartered away his birthright, and now has to suffer for it. Unless you are sure that the child's sympathy is wrong and mistaken, you should never let him have the vague notion which so many grown people have about this story, that God's standard of right is somehow different from theirs.

§ 6. *The Sin and Punishment of Each*

What was Isaac's sin? Not quite sure. I think it was that though he knew God's will about Jacob, he tried to give the blessing to Esau, his favourite. Otherwise it is hard to see why, when he discovered the trick, he did not reverse his blessing, and in fierce anger curse Jacob. What did he do? "Trembled very exceedingly," and confirmed the blessing (*v.* 33); trembled probably with awe and fear, as he saw God's purpose conquering them all, making one sin overthrow another.

Esau's sin we know. What was Rebekah's and Jacob's sin? Doing evil that good might come. Probably they both knew God's purpose. Perhaps their excuse to themselves was—"We want God's will to be done. God's

149

will is in danger. We had better tell lies and deceive to accomplish it." Some people are tempted to that still, and say or do things not quite straight, or not quite charitable, "in the interests of religion." Does that make it less wrong? No; God will hate and punish it just the same. When you are in doubt about your conduct, be sure always that the one only way to accomplish God's will is to do the right at any cost, to follow your highest instincts, your noblest aspirations. Never can you please God by ignoble means.

God punished them all. How? Esau lost the birthright that he could not appreciate. Isaac had his home peace destroyed. Rebekah never again saw her darling son. Jacob, the deceiver, was deceived again and again by Laban, as we shall see, and spent twenty-one years of hard labour and banishment. Never fancy that because you trust in God He will let you commit sin without suffering for it. Would that be real love? God has higher ambition for you than merely to make you comfortable and happy. He must make you good at any cost—the rod, the scourge, the pain, the increased temptation, the evil consequences of many kinds—that is the great loving discipline of God. He is too wise and good to rest satisfied till He destroy and burn that evil out of our lives.

§ 7. God's Purpose Accomplished

Is not it wonderful? In spite of all the wrong-doing, and unbelief and worldliness, and lying and trickery appearing in this story, God's will got done after all.

Oh, that is one's comfort and hope for this poor evil world, with men lying and tricking, and sinning and failing—God is above all. He will help them, or punish, or do what is best for them; but His good purposes cannot be spoiled by them.

> "God's in His heaven:
> All's right with the world."

NOTE ON "ELECTION"

I

This story of the election of Jacob and the rejection of Esau is to many thoughtful teachers a puzzle and perplexity, especially when they read it in connection with St. Paul's comment in Romans ix. 10-13. There is, though they do not like to put it into words, a tacit suspicion of arbitrary favouritism on the part of God; and this spoils the heartiness of their teaching, and hides from them the grandeur of God's purposes in election. In a lesser degree this difficulty has been running through the previous Lessons—the election of Abraham, the election of the Israelite nation, etc. Therefore it is just as well that it should be forced into prominence here.

The difficulty, of course, mainly arises from false traditions, a false doctrine of election. Some of us have been brought up in such traditions, and have learned that election of one implies reprobation of others—that God sent certain babies into this world destined to eternal heaven, and certain others destined to eternal

151

hell; not for any good or evil in them, but for His own glory, to magnify His power. As Burns has put it, with his terrible sarcasm, in *Holy Willie's Prayer:* —

> "O Thou, with whom all goodness dwell,
> Wha, as it pleasest best Thysel',
> Sends ane to heaven and ten to hell,
> All for Thy glory,
> And na for any good or ill
> They've done afore Thee."

If that were the Bible teaching about Jacob and Esau, it would indeed be a terrible lesson to teach. Let us be thankful that the deeper study of Scripture, and the fuller enlightenment of the Christian conscience thereby, have made such teaching now for ever impossible, and that our most thoughtful commentators boldly assert that it has no warrant at all from any word in the Bible.

Why, then, do I think it necessary to write this note? Because the recoil from the false doctrine is doing grave harm in leading some of our teachers to ignore plain statements of inspired Scripture, and in leaving a vague impression that God has no definite plan for individual lives. In refuting the false doctrine of predestination and election, it was necessary to seek for the true. For, whether we like it or not, predestination and election run through all Scripture. Through the Old and New Testaments alike we are told of certain persons, or races, or Churches chosen especially by the Almighty, "elect according to the foreknowledge of God." We find something very like this in secular history, too, even in the ordinary life around us to-day. Everywhere we meet the mysterious fact that God gives special gifts to some which He withholds from others. Some are born to beauty, to position, to influence and power; one great genius stands out in the midst of an ignorant family; one nation is gifted with special characteristics which raise it over other nations; and so on.

In secular history, however, it does not disturb our consciences. We realize that all life is a great plan of God slowly working itself out for the blessing of the world. And therefore we see nothing strange in the fact that He should elect, predestinate, and allot higher and lower places to individuals, for the accomplishment of His beneficent purposes. No general could win a victory, no prime minister could carry on a government, no musician could perform a great oratorio, if there were no plan, no electing individuals, and allotting to them their parts. It seems quite reasonable that God should do this, and it does not trouble us with any sense of unfairness, for we see that great endowment means great responsibility, and that the greater endowment of the few is for the good of the many, and does not preclude the many in their lesser endowment from living happy and holy lives.

II

If we could see that something of this kind is true also of God's election of men in Bible history, our difficulties on the subject would soon pass away. The subject of election is a great mystery. There are depths in the secret purposes of God which can never be

THE BOOK OF GENESIS

fathomed by our puny minds. Therefore there must be no glib talking of it, as if any child could explain what it really means.

Yet, on the other hand, it is not an insoluble mystery. Clear and distinct runs one clue-line through it—"The Judge of all the earth must do right." Holding this clue-line, much can be learned of it by careful study of the Bible. Let me indicate briefly what careful students have learned. In this short note I cannot give proofs or processes of reasoning. I can merely point out the lines on which our teachers may proceed in investigating the subject for themselves in the Bible.

First, as to what it *does not mean*—

1. It does NOT mean that God ever sent any baby into the world predestined to eternal destruction. The special calling, and election, and blessing of some does not in any way prejudice the eternal prospects of those who are not so called. We do not need nowadays to prove such things. Merely to remind the student that God is good, and to ask that he should think over certain questions, such as, for example, how a great soul like St. Paul's could have spoken of election with such a solemn joy and enthusiasm if it meant that, or how he could, in the next breath, tell us so gladly that "God willeth *all men* to be saved."

2. It does NOT mean that men and women are acted on irrespective of their own will and co-operation. They are not like mere marionettes on a stage, with the Almighty Ruler pulling the strings. St. Paul warns the elect Christian Church: "Be not high-minded, but

fear . . . lest God also spare not thee." He bids men "make their calling and election sure," and he hints the possibility of at least conceiving that he himself might be a castaway. It is a glorious and inspiriting thing to feel that some are "elect" to co-operate with God, chosen by His eternal love and wisdom to accomplish something in the world. But the elect must will to co-operate with the will of God. If they do, there should come the glad comfort that God's purpose is behind them, and that "He who has begun a good work in them will perform it unto the end."

3. It does NOT mean necessarily an election to prosperity, and comfort, and happiness. Look at the most prominent of the elect mentioned in the Bible. They are the strugglers and sufferers, the men who, in pain, and loneliness, and helpless clinging to God, are learning God's deepest lessons wherewith to enrich the world. Let that thought come to you as you teach this story of Jacob and Esau, when you hear the children say, "It was not fair to poor Esau that Jacob should be the elect." I doubt very much if Esau would have accepted such an election, with the terrible discipline needed to change the tricky, selfish Jacob of youth into the noble-hearted old Israel, the "Prince with God." Esau had everything that he cared for—hunting, and fighting, and eating, and drinking, and wives, and children, and the honours of the world. His rejection from God's plan for the race did not necessarily mean his rejection from heaven if he grew fitted for it. But look at Jacob, the elect, with his terrible life-discipline—the long exile, the dead young wife, the lost Jacob, the lonely old age, the grey

hairs going down in sorrow almost to the grave. There is surely little for worldly men to envy in that weary discipline by which the mean and false is purged out of elect souls, to make them fit for God's purpose.

III

If these be what it *does not* mean, can we get any glimpse of what election *does* mean? Some little glimpse we can. I have already pointed out to you, in teaching about the election of Abraham, that it was not for his own sake, but for that of the world at large. "I will bless thee," said God, "and thou shalt be a blessing." "In thee and in thy seed shall all the families of the earth be blessed." That is, the calling and election of Abraham WAS FOR THE SERVICE OF OTHERS.

That first recorded instance of "election"—the call of Abraham—strikes the key-note of all. As you go through the history of the elect souls in the Bible, you will see that it consistently and throughout affirms "that when God calls or separates one man to Himself, it is for the good of other men; that when He selects one family, it is that through it all the families of the earth should be blessed; that when He chooses one nation, it is for the welfare of all nations—salvation being *of* the Jews, but *for* the Gentiles as well; that when He elects and establishes a Church, it is for the spiritual benefit of the whole world. No man, no family, no nation, no Church, possesses any gift, any privilege, any superior capacity or power for its own welfare alone, but for the common advantage, the general good."

Are you beginning now to get a glimpse into the reason of St. Paul's enthusiasm about this doctrine of God's election? Are you beginning to see that it may be a nobler thing than Augustine or John Calvin imagined—a something more worthy of the All-Just, All-Merciful, All-Generous Father of all men? I have not been foolish enough to attempt an explanation of this mystery. I have but offered you a few hints to guide you, and to save you from unworthy views of God. You will still find difficulties connected with the subject; but if you take as the central thought ELECT FOR THE SERVICE OF OTHERS, and find out how far that is taught you in the Bible, the worst of your moral difficulties about the doctrine of election will gradually pass away, and instead of them will come the ennobling thought that there is a great, blessed purpose of God to which the elect minister, God's plan is to use the few to influence the many. Those elected to the highest gifts of capacity, genius, beauty, position, influence, are by that very election bound to the service of the rest. Those to whom the highest measure of God's grace comes to make them noble and lovable are those who can most deeply influence others to be so too. The great elect body, the Christian Church, is elected for the universal reconciling of the world to God. God help us all to realize the grandeur and moral beauty of this election, and to live worthy of that high calling to which we, as members of the Church, are called. *Noblesse oblige.*

QUESTIONS FOR LESSON XIV

Did the marriage of Isaac and Rebekah continue as beautifully as it began?

Why do you think this?

Who were their two sons?

Tell fully the story of Jacob deceiving his blind father.

What did Esau feel about this?

What do you think of Esau's character?

What do you think of Jacob in his youth?

What of him in his old age?

Why the difference?

Have you any notion as to meaning of "election"?

THE VISION AT BETHEL

Genesis XXVII. 41 to XXIX. 15

§ 1. *The Flight*

Esau hated Jacob. Why? Question briefly on last Lesson. So Rebekah cleverly planned that Jacob should be sent away out of danger. For how long? (*v.* 44). How did she plan it? (*v.* 46). Think of her thoughts turning back to the old home of her girlhood, that she had left one bright morning about fifty years ago, to be Isaac's bride. And she would picture her son arriving, and seeing the dear old place, and staying for a few days, and coming back to tell her how it all looked. Poor loving, sinning, planning mother! She never counted on her son so quickly falling in love with his cousin, and declining to come back. She never counted on her brother Laban being as clever as herself. So the years went on, and she waited and waited for him who never came. And at last died without ever seeing him again. So, perhaps, was she punished for her deceit. Tell me Isaac's charge to Jacob? and the blessing? (*v.* 4). Meaning of "the blessing of Abraham"? So you see the faith in God's promise firm still.

Now, see lonely Jacob leaving home for the first time—very lonely thing. Ever been away from home yourself? Do you know of anyone leaving home for the first time to go amongst strangers? Had Jacob anything worse than loneliness? Probably terrified lest Esau should catch him up. He knew well he deserved punishment. He knew he had tricked Esau, and deceived his father, and so the going away all the sadder. He had been very mean and dishonourable, and wicked, and deserved no kindness from God or man. Yet, don't you think he must have been sorry? Why? Yes. God's coming to comfort and encourage and bless him. He would scarcely do that to one impenitent. When you are very lonely, or sorrowful, or penitent for sin, that is God's favourite time to draw near. Give instances? (Lamentations iii. 55; Acts xxiii. 11; xxvii. 24, etc.) Many have at such times learned to love and trust and yield themselves to God.

§ 2. *The Vision*

Probably some days travelling. Now night drawing on, he finds himself on a great bleak moorland among the hills of Bethel. Probably had often heard of the place from his grandfather. Why? (xii. 8). Perhaps found the old altar, and settled down there to sleep. It was a wild spot, the sloping ground strewn with slabs of white rock, with the big crags standing irregularly around, like old Druid remains in our day. Looking at it sleepily, it might well seem like a great staircase of rock and crag reaching from earth to sky. You know the way that waking scenes weave themselves into dreams? Probably the whole scene wove itself into this dream, which was sent to encourage him, the dream of the wondrous giant staircase, with God at the top of it, and the angels of God ascending and descending between God and himself. Thus God revealed Himself in the visions of the night to encourage and teach Jacob.

How would this encourage him? What would it mean? Angels coming down from God to help him; angels going up to tell God all about him. Probably it was his first direct dealing with God. His father and grandfather would have told him of such; therefore very solemn for him. Why did he specially want comfort and encouragement just now? Yes, loneliness, fear, conscience troubled, unknown future before him. Tell me God's three promises to him. When before similar promise given? (Genesis xiii. 15, 16). What was meant by "all the families of the earth shall be blessed"? Which was the promise to himself personally?

What new lesson about God did he learn? (xxviii. 16). "I knew it not." Can we learn it? We sometimes thus. We quite believe God is in church, or at a graveside, etc., but that God is in every place—in school, playground, road, street, mountain—that wherever we are, are the invisible stairs, whose one end is at every poor man's door, and its other end at the footstool of God—of that we are not so conscious. Yet it is true. At any moment we can dart up prayers to God. Always and everywhere the angels of God may be ascending and descending upon us.

What did our Lord once say about this? (John i. 51). To whom? This story was probably the portion Nathanael had just been reading "under the fig-tree," where he was at his devotions—the thought in his mind about angels. Hence, probably, Christ's allusion. Through Him is the eternal stairway between earth and heaven. He is the "mediator between God and man." Explain and dwell on this.

What did Jacob do in the morning to keep this glad vision in remembrance? I think we might call this Jacob's conversion—the beginning of the new high life which made him such a noble character afterwards. And I think it was caused by his being touched to the heart by God's undeserved goodness to him. Just when he had been so wicked, and was sorrowful for it, and lonely, God came, and helped, and forgave, and comforted him. No amount of fear of punishment, or hope of reward, can touch men's hearts like that. That is what should touch us all most, and make us love God. Jacob wants not to forget it, so sets up his pillar as a memorial. What two vows did he make? Those are good vows for each of you. Life will be a beautiful and blessed thing if you make them. In every decision between right and wrong all your life say: "The Lord shall be my God." In every increase of money, and power, and ability, and influence, say: "I have got it from God; I will surely use part of it for Him." Everyone should give a fixed proportion of his money. And everyone, too, should give a portion of his time, and thought, and energy for

God's work. World full of social evils—drunkenness, pauperism, child neglect, misery of every kind. Why? Partly because the clever busy men and women give little thought and energy to cure it. Too busy about themselves and their families. If people gave to Christ's business of helping the helpless even a tenth of the time, and thought, and energy they give to their own business, we should have a very much better world. If people gave to increase religion in the world, a tithe of the money, or prayer, or thought that they give to their own affairs, Christ's Kingdom would soon come. Remember that God's plan is to help men and women only by means of other men and women; and if these will not help, the misery and wrong must remain. So if you would make life better for others, God must be your God, and you must give a share of all your powers to God's work on earth.

§ 3. *The Meeting with Rachel*

Now, with his new-formed resolve, Jacob starts afresh on his journey. Tell me of the meeting at the well. Tell of any other story like it in Old Testament. Lesson XIII. And so Jacob finds, in spite of all his badness, that God has for him a still greater happiness than he had ever hoped for. What? The love of his young cousin Rachel. I think she must have been both beautiful and good, if we are to judge from her son Joseph, and if it be true, as people say, that a boy inherits his qualities mainly from his mother. At any rate, we know she was very dear to Jacob. Not merely that he loved her at first sight, but deeply and enduringly. How is it expressed? (xxix. 20).

Don't you think God was very good to Jacob? Was it because Jacob deserved it? Do you think He is good to you? Tell me some of the good things you have to be thankful for. Is it that you deserve them? I think if we counted up all God's goodness, we should not have time for grumbling any more. A dear old man, long since dead, said to the writer long ago: "If you want to be happy, never rise up from prayer any day without thanking God for something; and if you can't think of anything to thank Him for at the moment, say the General Thanksgiving." Could not some of you take that old man's advice?

QUESTIONS FOR LESSON XV

Jacob had to leave home. Why?

Where did he go to?

Tell his dream about angels on the stairs.

What vows did he make then?

Here comes another story like that of old Eliezer and Rebekah. Tell it.

What trick did Laban play on Jacob?

Show how in all this new experience Jacob was being punished and yet trained to be better.

LESSON XVI

A CRITICAL DAY

Genesis XXXII. and XXXIII. to v. 10

Teacher should sketch in briefly the events between last Lesson and this. Tell briefly that many years have elapsed since story of meeting Rachel at well; how Jacob worked to win her, and was tricked by Laban, as he himself had tricked his old father, Isaac; how Laban had treated him unfairly again and again, till at last he determined to fly from him with his wives and cattle; how Laban pursued him, and how they parted at Mizpah.

Now we come to the most critical day of all Jacob's life—morning, evening, midnight, all full of exciting events. What was the most important time before this? Probably that of the Bethel vision, the offer of God's friendship from the great rock stairs while the angels ascended and descended upon it. But now a far greater day.

§ 1. Morning

First, in the early morning he parted from Laban, and started to continue his journey to Canaan. He was rid of one enemy, Laban, but the dread of a far more dangerous one was on his heart. Who? How do you know? (*vv.* 3, 4). Yes, he had sent the messengers perhaps some days before, and now he was anxious and frightened, expecting every moment to meet them on the road, or perhaps to meet Esau with his warrior band. Dangerous road, and helpless condition, to meet a hostile chief. Women, children, cattle, farm servants, very helpless. And at any moment he might see the spears of Edom flashing over the hill. What *did* he see instead? (*v.* 1). A wondrous sight—a bright procession, probably of warrior angels, coming down the mountain side to meet him. We are told very little of them.

But it seems likely God gave vision for encouragement. Refer to Elisha's servant in 2 Kings vi. 17, and Psalms xxxiv. 7: "The angel of the Lord encampeth," etc. It would remind Jacob of a scene twenty-five years earlier (*ch.* xxviii). Are they always about us? (reference, O. T. and N. T.) Perhaps by a slight change in our eyes or in our minds they would become visible at once. Wonderful, glorious, solemn thing this life of ours, with God's presence and God's angels everywhere around.

§ 2. Evening

The messengers at last! "Well, what tidings from Esau?" Very serious tidings! "The chieftain of Seir is coming with 400 warriors after him." What did Jacob think of Esau's purpose? Friendly? Hostile? Evidently the messengers thought so too. And probably it was so. We can't be sure.

We find Esau afterwards kindly and generous—but did not something happen that might have changed his purpose? (*vv.* 9-13). Who can tell the changes in men's purposes every day, through other men's prayers? Possible that Esau did not mean slaughter; but possible, too—nay, probable—that he did, and that by that prayer he was saved from being a murderer, and Jacob and his family from being all slain.

Now look at this prayer. Notice that he first does all he can himself. "God helps those who help themselves." Don't you think from it that Jacob was becoming a better man since we last met him? It is a simple, humble, beautiful prayer. Show me in it his humility? his belief in God? his claiming God's promises? Does it show any comfort because he was in the path of duty? (*v.* 9). "Thou saidst to me, Return," etc. That is a great comfort always. If ever you are in doubt between two courses, never mind the consequences, but ask—which way lies duty? Which is the higher, nobler? Which is likely to be God's will? Then, even if trouble and vexation come of that course, you can feel like Jacob: "I tried to do Thy will; Thou saidst to my conscience, Do it; therefore I can leave it all to Thy care." So Jacob. Then, probably calmed by the prayer, he cleverly arranges his presents for Esau. Show the cleverness (*vv.* 14-21).

§ 3. Midnight

Now a very mysterious story. Don't quite understand
it. Poor Jacob in great dread. Where was Jacob? Who
with him? Where were they all?

If you were in a great fright, should you like to be
alone on a dark night? Why did he? Perhaps so troubled
he could not bear the chatter; probably because in
his great torture of soul he must be alone with God.
Remember similar case of our Lord (St. Matthew,
xxvi. 39). Now picture the lonely man sitting by the dark
rushing stream at midnight, thinking of his past, his
present, his dangerous future, praying to God, thinking
of God. Far in front he hears the noises dying away in
the distance as his people go farther away. At last he
rises to cross the river. Can he do it? Instantly he is
gripped in a powerful wrestler's grip. He is startled. He
wrestles. He can't overcome; but he won't give in. He
strains and struggles, and the great calm wrestler holds
him firmly still. A dread is creeping on him, a feeling
of the supernatural. No mortal man can this be who
is wrestling with him! Who can he be? Is it God? Is it
one of the angels he has seen? But still he won't give in.
And at last, as the dawn breaks, the mysterious being
can wait no more. He conquers. How? And instantly as
that nerve is touched the struggle is over, and the poor
helpless Jacob is clinging, instead of wrestling, clinging
to be held up from falling, crying out, "I will not let Thee
go, unless Thou bless me!" And then a wonderful thing
happens. *By this helpless clinging he conquers!* (*v.* 28).
And so a great lesson taught him. Not by his strength,

but by helpless clinging to God in his weakness, does man prevail with God.

I can't quite explain this wrestling. Don't quite understand it myself. Some people think it only meant eager wrestling with God in prayer. See what Hosea says (Hosea xii. 3). But that would not explain his being lamed as result of struggle. Who did Jacob think wrestled with him? (*v*. 30). We know too little of the mysteries of the Unseen to form any conjecture. But we believe the whole matter was of God. See angels with Abraham (xviii. 3), and the captain of Lord's host (Joshua *v*. 14). Remember that morning the host of bright angels on the hillside revealed to his sight. We can only guess. But we *know* that God meant to teach him a great lesson by it. And He means to teach us great lessons by it. Here is one:—

§ 4. Lesson

The great, calm, strong God is frequently wrestling with us. He wants to conquer. Why? For His own good? No, but for ours, to make us noble, to make us entirely yielded up to His will, that He may bless us utterly. And we poor fools keep struggling and wrestling. Our will has been allowed that wonderful power of holding out even against the Almighty God.

Do you remember ever wrestling thus, wanting your own will? Could He not force our will? But will He? Why not? Because He wants to gain us not as slaves, but as loving children. Sometimes He has to touch us as the angel did, with pain, and weakness, and disappointment, to break down the power of the opposition. A girl vain of her beauty, a boy proud of his popularity, men and women full of their ambitions. They don't want to give up God. Would like in a measure to serve Him, but not utterly. And He wants them to serve Him utterly. So the wrestle goes on. At last in love God has to touch the sinew. What does that mean? To touch that beauty or popularity, or ambition, or whatever made the strength of our opposition. But all in love, because He has much grander things for us, which He wants us to win. What? Love, truth, faithfulness, generosity, unselfishness—in a word, a noble character. And sometimes boys and girls, and men and women, in pain and vexation and disappointment, learn, at last, whom they have been wrestling with, and, clinging, in their weakness, cry: "Bless me, Lord! make me good at any cost! I will not let Thee go, except Thou bless me!" And so they, too, like poor Jacob, rise to be princes with God.

§ 5. Meeting with Esau

Have not time to read next chapter. Just look at it. We want to see answer to Jacob's prayer. Esau, in spite of all his unworthiness, had a great deal of good in him. I never yet saw a man that had not some. We were all made in the image of God, and the image has not been quite defaced in any man.

We don't know how much Jacob's prayer had to do with Esau's attitude, nor how much the angel hosts on the hillside, nor whether the strong wrestler, who had to go at the dawn, was going to meet Esau, and influence his heart.

All we know is that Jacob, in his terror of Esau's 400 men, met a generous, kindly brother and 400 soldiers, who would guard him, instead of killing him. And so we are glad. It helps us to believe that, though Esau was rejected from God's great purpose for the world, he was not rejected from God's love or God's heaven. It helps us to believe that he, too, became a better man. It helps us to believe in the power of prayer, and in the blessed guardianship of the angels of God.

And there is another lesson: "Fret not for to-morrow." Or, as old proverb says: "Don't cross the river till you come to it." Half the fretting in the world is for evils that never happen after all. Here was Jacob fretting for years at the thought of some day meeting Esau, whom he had wronged. Be sure it had worried him through many a sleepless night in Padan-aram. And now, after all his fretting, he finds there is nothing to fear. What does our Lord say of this? "Take no thought, i.e., fret not about to-morrow." Need not any man be afraid of the morrow? Yes; but if the life is given up to God in lowly penitence, even after doing wrong, we may trust God with the future. "Rest in the Lord and wait patiently for Him." "Fret not thyself for tomorrow." Live one day at a time. Here is a useful prayer for people who fret about the future:—

JUST FOR TO-DAY

(A Morning Prayer)

Lord, for to-morrow and its needs
    I do not pray;
Keep me, my God, from stain of sin,
    Just for to-day.

Let me both diligently work
    And duly pray;
Let me be kind in word and deed
    Just for to-day.

Let me be slow to do my will—
    Prompt to obey;
Help me to sacrifice myself
    Just for to-day.

Let me no wrong or idle word
    Unthinking say;
Set Thou a seal upon my lips
    Just for to-day.

Cleanse and receive my parting soul,
    Be Thou my stay;
Bid me, if to-day I die,
    Go home to-day.

So, for to-morrow and its needs
    I do not pray;
But keep me, guide me, hold me, Lord,
    JUST FOR TO-DAY.

QUESTIONS FOR LESSON XVI

This is a most critical day in Jacob's life.

What happened in the (1) morning, (2) evening, (3) midnight?

What other time had he seen angels?

Show that Esau too was becoming a better man.

Illustrate here the proverb "Never cross a bridge until you come to it."

What does our Lord say about this "not fretting for the morrow," and why does He say we are not to fret?

What is the spiritual meaning of "wrestling with God"?

LESSON XVII

JOSEPH—GOD'S LEADING

Genesis XXXVII. and XXXIX. to v. 7

The story of Jacob now ceases for the present. He has grown an old man, and by God's discipline a good man, which he certainly was not at first. He will come before us again at the close of this story. But for the present the inspired historian passes away from him to talk about one of his sons. The probable reason we shall see as we go on.

§ 1. The Boy Joseph

We have to spend some time with the story of Joseph, so I want you to get to really know him, and try to enter into his thoughts and feelings. How old was he at this time? Do you think he was a handsome boy? (xxxix. 6). Was he religious? (xxxix. 2-5). Was he a lonely boy, or had he plenty of friends? Was anybody in the encampment fond of him?

I have sometimes pictured him to myself a tall, handsome boy, dressed in his beautiful robe with its border of gold and colours at the neck and sleeves. A clever boy, with his father's cleverness, as well as his mother's beauty. And yet a lonely boy, amongst all his rough companions, whose thoughts were so different from his. All the more lonely because his mother was dead. A motherless boy is a very lonely boy. I picture him sometimes when his brothers were very cruel to him, sitting out in the pasture fields, and letting the old memories rise up to him. He could remember his childhood in Laban's pastures, where his father was the manager. He could remember one day, when somebody seized him and put him on a big camel, when they were all running away secretly from Haran, and the excitement of feeling that Laban was pursuing. Then the terrible fright about his uncle Esau coming to kill them, and the caravan hurrying off in the early dawn, and stopping when they missed his father, and their wonder when he limped up to them lamed for life, but with a strangely serious, solemn look on his face. And clearest of all his memories stood out one terrible day when they stopped on their march, and his brothers and the drovers and servants whispered together, and his father was distracted with grief, and they told the poor boy that his young mother was dying. That was a terrible day to him and his father, the two who loved her best in all that company. It was a tie between them ever after. The old man loved Joseph, and confided in him more than in any of his other sons; and all the days of his life the old father was first in Joseph's thoughts. He knew more of his father's secret struggles and God's dealings with him than his unsympathetic elder brothers or the child

175

Benjamin could possibly know. I feel pretty sure that when they were passing Bethel, Jacob showed him the altar he had built, and told him about the great stairs whose top reached to heaven. Perhaps it was there that his heart first thrilled with the solemn resolve of his life that God should be his God, too, for ever and ever.

§ 2. The Dreamer

Now we have got in some degree acquainted with Joseph, tell me two reasons why his brothers hated him. What do you think of his telling tales of his brothers? Is it not a mean thing to tell tales of others? Perhaps Joseph was wrong. Yet I don't know. In after days we find he knew well enough when to hold his tongue.

We know that some of these brothers were fearfully wicked, and perhaps out on the lonely pastures the poor boy was often startled and shocked at their abominable conduct, and found it necessary to tell. Do you think it was wise or right of Jacob to dress him in more beautiful clothes than the others? Do you remember that sort of favouritism in Jacob's own boyhood? Did much good come of it?

Now tell me first dream? Meaning? Second dream? Meaning? How did his father like it? (*v.* 10). Yet he thought seriously about it (*v.* 11). Now tell me the story of journey to Dothan? Was it dangerous? Why? What did they say about "this dreamer and his dreams"? Yet God had sent those dreams to show His great purpose for Joseph. Is it possible to hinder God's purposes? These men tried. What result? That they helped them on instead. How? Wonderful about God's purposes, that no opposition is the least use in hindering them.

Poor Joseph! Little he thought of his brethren's evil intention. First, to kill him. Who persuaded them not? Then they found one of those great pits that shepherds dig in the East to let the waters run in in rainy weather, to be used in drought. It was covered with a big slab. Fancy being left to starve to death in that horrid, slimy place, with crawling things all about, in the darkness. Many a poor boy would go mad with terror. Poor Joseph cried out, and besought mercy. We are not told that here. How do you know it? Because his cries and agony tortured his cruel brothers' conscience for years and years; and in their terrible fright in Egypt many years afterwards they whispered it to each other (xlii. 21). A good thing that God has given conscience such power to torture.

How did he escape that death? Great central road to Egypt runs by Dothan. The brothers saw dust rising, and heard the shouts of a great caravan. Often saw them bringing merchandise and slaves to Egypt. "Ha! This is much better. We need not murder the boy. Sell him. Get twenty pieces of silver for him. Good price got for slaves in Egypt." Was it much better for poor Joseph? Not much, it would seem. Egyptian slavery a terrible thing. Might be sold in the market to some very cruel person. Poor boy! how he cried and prayed, and besought mercy. All no use. Nobody cared. Perhaps it seemed to the poor lad that even God did not care.

§ 3. God's Purposes

Did God care? He heard the cries and prayers in the pit. He saw the boy's agony when tied in the slave-gang. Yet He did not save him. Was God cruel? Was He indifferent? Why not save him? Ah, because that was just the very way to lead to the highest good for Joseph, and his father, and brethren, and the Israelite nation, and the whole world afterwards. Poor foolish men and women still cry out against God, and say He does not care; and God has to bear all that, and still He goes on guiding their lives patiently and wisely for their good.

I want you to think about the way God's purposes get fulfilled by what seem just chance events. Do we not all feel ourselves quite free to do good or do evil? Do we not know that everybody else is so too? We never know what people may choose to do. It would seem at first as if all went by chance in the world, and that God could not possibly make any plan which He could count on being fulfilled. Yet somehow He is able to leave every man free to do what he likes, and yet to take care that His own wonderful plans for human life are carried out.

God told Abraham of His great project for the Jews. What? To be a great nation; to be the helpers and teachers of religion for the world; to be the nation of whom Christ should come. God had planned for them, as part of their training, that they should be slaves in Egypt (xv. 13). Perhaps because they had to be somewhere out of Canaan while growing into a nation, and also that they had to learn a good deal from the wise Egyptians—the wisest nation on earth. Whatever the reason, it was part of God's plan for them. And now here we have a story of family quarrels, and cruel brothers, and merchants passing by chance, and buying a slave-boy. It seems to have nothing to do with God's purpose. It seems all mere chance. Was it? Tell me again God's message to Abraham 200 years before (xv. 13, 14). 200 years, and everybody doing what they liked; not in the least thinking about or trying to help God's purpose. And yet how wonderfully it is coming right, though it seems to men all chance. Where did these slave-dealers take Joseph to? Yes; and then there was a slave sale, and the boy stood bound amongst the other slaves, and rough men were examining him, and feeling his muscle, and haggling about his price, when suddenly there rode in one of the great officers of the king. He looks round the market, and his eye falls on the handsome boy standing near a post. "What is the price of that boy? Send him up to my house." And so the next step is taken, that is to bring Joseph near to the King of Egypt, and by-and-by to bring all his family down there to live.

Thus God's purposes were being fulfilled then, and are being fulfilled now. We see only the chance things happening. The Bible writers could see God standing behind all, and guiding everything, even the wickedness of bad men, to work out His purpose. What is God's purpose for you? I don't know all of them, but I know one—that is, that you are to make a good, true, faithful servant of His; and He will guide all your life to accomplish that, and nobody but yourself can hinder its coming to pass. Is not your life a grand and hopeful thing thus guided by God?

QUESTIONS FOR LESSON XVII

What age was Joseph when he first appears in story?

A lonely boy—why?

His two dreams and their meaning?

What happened at Dothan?

Three reasons why his brothers hated him?

Who was Potiphar?

Show God's leading in all this trouble.

LESSON XVIII

JOSEPH IN PRISON

Genesis XXXIX. v. 20 to end, and XL.

Recapitulate briefly last Lesson. Remind of God's purpose for the whole family of Israel, that they should go down to Egypt to be trained and disciplined. Remind of purpose for Joseph, and for every man, that he should grow to be a brave, faithful servant of God. Watch the accomplishing of this purpose. What was our last sight of Joseph? Carried off with fettered limbs to Potiphar's house.

§ 1. *Disgraced*

Now comes new scene to-day. Several years have passed, and the boy, now grown to be a young man, is leaving Potiphar's house, *and again with fettered limbs.* He is a prisoner, disgraced and shamed, and they are hurrying him to the State prison, where the State criminals are kept. Has he committed some crime? Has he forgotten God? Not he! but his master's wife hates him, and has told a terrible lie about him, and Potiphar believes it, and the brave young slave holds his tongue. He will not hurt his kindly master by telling that his wife is a liar and a wicked woman. He will bear his wrong silently.

Potiphar had been very good to him. He saw that in the midst of schemers and liars this Hebrew boy was honourable and true and faithful; and step by step he advanced him over all the servants, and trusted him with his whole house and all that was in it (xxxix. 6). Why was Joseph so faithful and honourable? (xxxix. 2). Yes; because he was a religious boy—because "the Lord was with him." No man could deprive him of that friendship of God. Men could rob him of home and father and freedom. No man could rob him of character—of God. He held fast by God all along. He knew that he belonged to God; that he was made in God's image and likeness; that he was meant to walk Godward, with head erect, and not crawl in the mud, and eat dirt like the serpent. That was what made a man of him, as it will of every boy who learns the same lesson. And because Joseph had learned that, he had faced his trouble and loneliness and hard work like a man. He was God's servant, not merely Potiphar's. He could be prompt and faithful and diligent; he could serve God in Potiphar's house as well as in his old Syrian home. Other servants might work to win Potiphar's praise, or escape Potiphar's whip; he would work for sake of right, of duty, of God. That was why Potiphar trusted him; that was why, as the old Wycliffe Bible puts it (*ch.* xxxix. *v.* 2), "The Lord was with Joseph, and he was a luckie fellowe."

§ 2. *In Prison*

But why then did God let him be sent to prison when innocent? Does not God always reward men who try to be good? Yes; and comfort and praise and good fortune usually come to them; but in God's sight comfort and praise and good fortune are not the highest rewards for right-doing.

What is *God's great reward for right-doing? A deeper love of right-doing.* I want you to repeat this three times, and try to remember it always. It explains a great many mysteries of life. I think Joseph must have learned this, or at least guessed it. Else I don't know how he bore up so well. Think of him in that prison, with the shame and dishonour, with the fetters and the filth, and the confinement, and the degraded companions. There he lay for seven years—the best years of his brave young life. If ever a man had excuse to lose heart, distrust God, and go wrong, he had. He had tried to be good at home long ago, and yet he was sold as a slave. He had tried to bear up still and be faithful to God, and to resist all sorts of temptation in Potiphar's house. He had held his tongue, and trusted God when falsely accused; and yet here he was eating out his heart in a filthy prison, and with no chance of ever getting out. How could he have kept his trust in God? I think he must surely have guessed the lesson that I want you to remember. (Repeat it again for me, one by one; then the whole class.)

What a beautiful way he tried of comforting himself! What was it? To try to amuse and cheer and comfort the other prisoners (*ch.* xl. 6, 7). The keeper of the prison had found out, too, what Potiphar had found out about Joseph's religion (xxxix. *v.* 21), and he left his cell open, and took his word of honour that he would not run away. He knew well he could trust him. And so Joseph used his freedom to help and comfort others. Is it a good plan? Yes; if ever you are misunderstood or slandered, if ever you are suffering in any way, the grandest way to get comfort is to go off and comfort others. Say to yourself: "Never mind my little troubles; others are worse off. I'll go and help them and comfort them." And God's reward will surely come in peace and comfort to yourself, and a new interest in life. That was Joseph's way. Better still, that was our Lord's way. The very night before He was wrongfully murdered, He spent in comforting His poor frightened disciples (St. John xiv. 1). Let not your heart be troubled, etc.

§ 3. *God's Purpose Again*

Now tell me about the two prisoners from the palace that got into the State prison. Who? What had Joseph to do with them? Tell me their talk with him. Tell me the first dream and interpretation. The second? Joseph's request to the chief butler? (*v.* 14). Did he remember it? Poor Joseph! think of his hopes day after day, as he looked through the prison bars for a message from his friend. But his friend was so busy about his grapes and his wines and the delight of his escape, that he had quite forgotten the poor lonely Hebrew lad. And so two years passed by, and life grew very hard. What reminded the butler at last? Tell me of Pharaoh and his dreams, and how Joseph's name is thought of.

Can you see now, as in last Lesson, how all these chance events were bringing about God's purposes? (1) State one purpose. That Israel should go down into Egypt, to be there prepared for their future. Here is Joseph coming in close contact with Pharaoh, about to be made a ruler of the kingdom, and here is the famine coming that will force his brethren to come down. We can only guess yet. We must watch how it all works out as the story goes on. (2) Now what was God's purpose for Joseph himself, and for every man in the whole wide world? Was this being accomplished? Yes. He was growing patient, and noble, and brave, and gentle, and unselfish, by means of the terrible discipline of these prison years. That might not have been the result in every man. But God was watching him, and training him, and making him strong through struggle. Like boys in a gymnasium, or training for races, etc. The training that hardens the muscles is very tiring, and often painful; but the trainer never spares for that. (3) What is God's purpose for you? To make you good at any cost of struggle and difficulty. He longs to make you brave and strong and holy. Therefore when He lets temptations come, and vexations and hard school lessons, etc., think of the great loving Trainer trying in every way to form splendid character in you, and pray to Him: "Lord, at any cost of trouble or difficulty make me good."

QUESTIONS FOR LESSON XVIII

Why did Potiphar trust Joseph and promote him?

What is God's chief reward for right-doing?

How did Joseph comfort himself in prison?

Tell the dreams of the chief butler and baker.

How did his acquaintance with these prisoners influence Joseph's career?

LESSON XIX

FROM THE PRISON TO THE STEPS OF THE THRONE

Genesis XLI. 14 to end

§ 1. *The Man Who Forgot*

Where did we leave Joseph? He had been in that prison for years already when he interpreted the chief butler's dream. You remember his request to the chief butler? Poor Joseph! Can't you imagine him on that birthday of the king? The whole city of Memphis was bright with music and colour, and joyous processions, and he could only just get a glimpse of it through the bars and wonder if he should ever be free again. His friend, the chief butler, was just going out; but Joseph could not go out. He could only beseech his friend to remember. Can't you imagine the man promising, in the joy of his liberation: "Of course I will remember you, Joseph. You have been a true friend to me, and I will not forget it. I have influence with the king and with Potiphar. Be quite sure that I will try to get you set free." And how the big doors closed behind him, and

187

the poor lad's heart was lighter for that promise, and how he waited and waited, hoping against hope, as the days passed into weeks, and the weeks into years, till all hope was gone. What had happened? (xl. 23). Ah, that forgetting by selfish people! The world is very sad for it. The friend forgotten by the friend; the poor old mother, sitting at home, listening for the postman's knock, for the letter which her boy had promised when he left home. "Be sure I'll write, mother, every week. I shan't forget you." Yet he did not remember, but forgot. Never let that be so with you. Ask God to keep you from selfish forgetting, which makes so much sadness in life.

Poor Joseph! in spite of all his trust in God, I am sure he had often his fits of black despondency, especially after his friend had forgotten him. He knew of many a man forgotten and left to rot in those prisons (cf. stories of the Bastille). I should not wonder if he sometimes said to himself, "Has God, too, forgotten me? Does God care?" I know many people who in troubles thus doubt at times. Now, if Joseph could see what was going to happen, would he have fretted? You can see it, and you know he had no cause to fret. But poor Joseph did not see it then. I am pretty sure he often looked back in after years, and said to himself, "How good and kind God was all the time! What a fool I was to distrust Him! Why, every one of my troubles was for good after all! If my brothers had not thrown me into the pit; if the Midianites had not bought me; if I had not been sold as a slave to Potiphar; if I had not been cast into prison, and met the chief butler—why, I might have missed all this happiness and usefulness. And when the butler forgot me, how miserable I was! But now I see it was for the best. If he had got me out of prison, I could not go back to Potiphar's house. I should have been sold as a slave to some farmer, or perhaps let go home to my father to live in obscurity all my life. And I should have missed the training and discipline of the prison, and the knowledge that came to me through my intercourse with the State prisoners, the knowledge about the king and the court, and the government, the very knowledge I wanted for my high position."

You will have your disappointments and reverses. Will you try to learn the lesson that all this taught to Joseph—that God has a plan for all men's lives, for yours and mine, as well as for Joseph's; for each of us the best of which we are capable; and that He will accomplish that plan for us if we do not hinder. But how can we find out and accomplish God's plan for us, if we do not exactly know that plan beforehand? Just as Joseph found it, and accomplished it. How? By always following your higher instincts—always obeying your nobler impulses—for they are always the indication of the guiding of the Holy Ghost. The one important thing is always to do right at any cost. Let that go on in your life, with the help of God, and then be certain that all else will go on in your life, too, that is in God's highest plan for you. What the Bible says is perfectly true for everyone in this class who will submit to God's leading, "I will inform thee, and teach thee in the way that thou shouldst go. I will guide thee with Mine eye."

§ 2. Before the King

The next scene is a very striking one. Try to picture in your minds a magnificent hall, the great Hall of Pillars, in the palace at Memphis; the king on his throne, the princes and rulers, and all the splendour of the court. Potiphar and his stern guard of kilted soldiers keeping the door.

They are just bringing Joseph in from the prison. Should not you think he would be very frightened coming before this great king? In his hands are life and death; in his face at the moment are anger, and impatience, and perplexity. Why does the king look so angry and impatient? He has dreamed, and his dream was repeated in another form to him. It has deeply impressed him, and he has just had in all the interpreters and magicians, and they have all failed him; and now he is utterly puzzled and vexed. Who thought of Joseph? Ah, the chief butler has remembered at last! Now, would you be frightened coming before this king, when all the wise men had failed? I don't think Joseph was. The story leaves the impression of quiet, simple dignity and ease. Why, do you think? I think he was so accustomed to the thought of a greater Presence, in which he always lived. Whose? So, too, the Baptist before Herod, and the Apostles before the Council (Acts iv. 13), all kept from fright and cringing by that "The Lord God, before whom I stand."

"I have heard," said the great king, "that you can interpret dreams. All my wise men have failed, and I want to see what you can do." I am going to ask you

190

Joseph's answer; but first let me remind you that this was a splendid chance for the poor prisoner. Interpreters of dreams had a high position. If, where they failed, Joseph succeeded, the king would think him cleverer than they, and probably give him a high post—make him a great man for life. He might say, "Yes, I can: I know more than all your magicians." Did he say it? What? (*v.* 16). "Not me, but God." You see he did not think the one important thing was that he himself should be promoted. But what? That God should be honoured. That God's will should be done. It is the old rule of his life. Follow the higher leading always, and leave the result with God. I wish I could get you all to learn that rule.

§ 3. *From the Prison to the Steps of the Throne*

Now tell me the dreams exactly as Pharaoh told them to Joseph. Now tell me exactly Joseph's interpretation. Who does he say had sent the dreams? (*v.* 28). Joseph knew that nations, no less than individuals, were God's care. Would it not be well if all our statesmen and politicians knew this, and acted on it as Joseph did? That was what made Joseph fit to be a great statesman and politician.

Who taught Joseph the meaning of the dreams? I suppose that was why he ventured on such daring as to give advice to the great king and court. Think of a young Hebrew slave, just out of gaol, doing this. See what courage comes from feeling oneself on God's side. What did he advise? And then he paused. What would happen to him? Would Pharaoh and the court be offended? Well, at any rate, he had tried to do right, and that was all that concerned him. What happened? Were they angry? What did the king say? (*vv.* 37-40). Do you think it strange? No. It is just the same to-day. In the long run the greatest influence always belongs to men like Joseph—men who are not thinking merely of themselves; to whom God, and right, and duty are the rule of life. People somehow feel that they can always trust themselves with such men. What a grand impression he made on Pharaoh! "A man in whom the Spirit of God is." I think it must have made the king wish to be religious too. Every one of us will make that impression on people if we are living close to Christ, and being brave, and true, and loving, and unselfish, as He wants us to be. And the more we are all like that, the more will careless people believe in religion, and seek it for themselves.

Tell me now all about Joseph's grandeur. Ah, God's promise is true. "Them that honour Me," etc. (1 Samuel ii. 30). Don't you wish poor old Jacob could have seen him on that day of his glory, moving like a king; a triumphal procession, with all the nobles in attendance, and all the people on their knees as he passed, and the shouting, and the music, and the waving of banners. Surely it must have been like a dream to him, who had been but a poor slave in the prison that morning. Don't you think his doubts and hard thoughts of God would vanish then?

§ 4. *A Religious Business Man*

With all this power and grandeur there came a great crush of work for Joseph. He had to have his council and his clerks, with their broad sheets of papyrus, and his buyers of corn, and overseers, and builders of granaries. And he had to travel north and south, and east and west, to inspect the works everywhere; and see after the draining, and ploughing, and building, and storing of corn. Sometimes he had to be away for weeks together, and then he would come back tired to his beautiful home and his young Egyptian wife, to get a few days' rest before he started again. I suppose he was busier than any man in Egypt. The whole responsibility was thrown upon him (see *v.* 55).

But from what we know of him already, what do you think about his prayers and his religion? Sometimes very busy people say they have not time for religion. Do you think Joseph made time for it? I am sure he did, even in the crush of his hardest work. Nay, I think that only for the help and refreshment of his religion he could not have got through the crush of that work at all. For religion, instead of taking away time and making hard work more weary, is just the thing to make work easier to do. And it is a great pity that men and women busy with the work of life, miss the peace and refreshment it would give. They go through life worried and tired, not refreshed themselves, and not refreshing to others.

Look at Joseph, busiest of all busy men. Do you remember how his father described him? (*ch.* xlix. 22).

"A fruitful bough *by a well,* whose branches run over the wall." *By a well.* Do you see the meaning? Amid the withered trees is one fresh and green. Why? Because down beside it lies the deep, cool well, and the roots run far down into its cool depths. Therefore the boughs are green, and the fruit rich. So Joseph's life. Can you explain? So with all. If busy people get habit of being with God, if they read their Bible, if they come every morning to consecrate the day, and every evening to ask forgiveness for the failures, and help and strength for the next day—that will keep the thought of God's presence with them in all their bustle and care; that will refresh and invigorate them: it will be like having the roots running into the cool, deep well.

QUESTIONS FOR LESSON XIX

Who was "the man who forgot"?

What made him remember?

Even this forgetting worked out well for Joseph?

Pharaoh's two dreams?

How did Joseph interpret them?

How did Pharaoh reward him?

What was his opinion of Joseph?

JOSEPH AND HIS BROTHERS

Genesis XLII., XLIII., XLIV.

I have taken the unusual course of putting these two Lessons into one. They are really one. I tried to make them into two; but it spoils the whole idea, and would be likely to make the teacher miss the point of the Lesson. But he must teach them as two.

Recapitulate last Lesson briefly. Point out that we are now passing over nine years to come to the beautiful story of Joseph's meeting his brothers. Teacher, study carefully *ch.* xlii. to xliii. 26. A mother with her children should spend several days over this story. A teacher in school must just use his discretion. Class cannot read sixty-four verses in the time. Best that teacher should read briefly and smartly with running comment, and sometimes passing over a few verses with a brief word of paraphrase. Or perhaps make the reading of these chapters with brief running comment the whole of one lesson.

§ 1. Joseph's Object

Story of Joseph and his brethren not enough appreciated or understood. Necessary to keep in mind: first, that Joseph was a man of great wisdom and sagacity, and compelled by his position to be a keen judge and tester of character; and, secondly, that, as the story proves, he had a very loving heart, and was deeply religious, and, therefore, was not likely to be spiteful or revengeful.

People sometimes say—How much kinder if Joseph had not so tormented his brothers, and made his father so anxious—if he had at once fallen on their necks, and forgiven them. What do *you* think? Before you answer remember what bad men they had been, and that in all these years they had never confessed their sin, but let old father mourn for Joseph as dead. Now, should Joseph have embraced and forgiven without knowing if they were sorry or not? Would it be good for them? Does God do it with us? Why not? Because it would do us great harm to pass over sin if we were impenitent.

Joseph had much more loving designs—designs such as God has towards all who do wrong; not first make them comfortable; but make them what? Good. So he had first to find out if they were different men from what they had been twenty years ago; and if not, to try to make them different. They must have penitent, changed hearts, else God could not forgive them. I don't know that he thought of all this the moment he saw them; probably not. Probably his plans grew as the days went on.

§ 2. How He Carried Out His Plan

Now follows the story. Seven years of plenty passed. Two years of famine had made the pinch of hunger felt in the nations around. Here first scene opens in to-day's story. Can you call up scene in your minds? Shut your eyes and try. Splendid hall in Memphis, the hall of the granaries, governor in chair of state, surrounded by bodyguard, and with a host of clerks and secretaries writing his orders; hall crowded with foreigners in their curious bright dresses. Now, I have that much of picture in my mind, have you?

Now, I see in the crowd ten rough-looking country-men staring around with wonder. The great civilization of Egypt has made a deep impression on them, the splendid buildings, the crowds of people, the trained soldiers, the swift chariots of red and yellow dashing through the streets. You know how simple country folk would be impressed. Just in the mood to fall down prostrate before the great lord of Egypt. Did they? (*v.* 6). What a start Joseph gets when he hears the voices! One moment his heart nearly stops beating, and the next he remembers—what? (*v.* 9). What dreams? How fulfilled now? How is it that he knows them and they don't know him?

He is watching and listening as they answer the usual questions of the clerks at the desk; and all the time he is thinking of the old days more than twenty years ago, and the dear old father, and merry little Benjamin playing with him in the fields. And one scene he surely thinks of—the last time he had seen those brothers. Oh, he could never forget that! I think he wants to remind them of it, and to trouble their consciences about it, and find out if they were sorry. With this in view, see how he treats them. Remember scene at Dothan. How the boy came to them helpless; they hated him, because they said he was a spy, and had brought to their father their evil report. How he pleaded and agonized (see *v.* 21). No use. "We'll soon stop his dreaming and his spying on us!" And down into the horrible black pit they forced him, and left him there in his terror to die, with the dark, and the damp, and the horrid, slimy, crawling things creeping on him. Now, he will bring it back to their memory. See his treatment of them (*vv.* 7-17). Speaks roughly, calls them spies, refuses to believe them, throws them into a dungeon, as if acting out the old scene again. (Illustration:—Story of *Hamlet*; secret murder; guilty pair not thinking of it. Hamlet gets players to act it out in dumb show on stage, till the conscience of guilty king nearly maddens him with remorse.)

Now, don't you think Joseph might stop? He had tried them. They were now frightened, and disturbed in conscience, and sorry for that old wickedness. Some people think he should have been satisfied here. What do you think? If you saw a wicked boy thinking of his sins when he was frightened at the darkness, or a selfish woman moved almost to tears by an earnest address, would you feel *quite sure* the life was changed to God? I should not. And Joseph would not either. He knew too much of people to believe in mere feelings and frights. He would think: "My brothers *may* be changed.

Probably they *are* changed. I know they are sorry, and their conscience is accusing them." But is being sorry the whole of repentance? No; must have a changed heart, a resolution to act differently in future. Joseph must feel satisfied that they never could do to Benjamin what they had done to him. For, you see, he noticed that Benjamin was not with them, and he would wonder why he was not; whether it was their jealousy and spite, or whether the old father, who knew them best, would be afraid to trust the boy with them.

So, in spite of his soft heart, though he was kinder, and let most of them go home, he had much testing to do still. What next? (*v.* 24). Why? Simeon was a very bad fellow (*ch.* xxxiv. 25, 30; *ch.* xlix. 5). I suspect he had been the ringleader in the attack on Joseph. If so, you see how it would still more frighten them; they would feel that God was punishing and bringing their sin to remembrance in a marvellous way. Don't you think Joseph's plan was working well?

So he sent them home frightened and perplexed, and very much disturbed in conscience. And he told them that Simeon must remain as a hostage to ensure their coming back with the young brother. But he did one very kind thing secretly to them (*v.* 25). So ends their first visit to Egypt. And before they come back there again, I have some questions to ask you.

§ 3. *God's Discipline*

Who had prompted Joseph thus to stir up his brothers' conscience? But does God care to do this for bad men? Thank God for it—yes. His care, and training, and discipline are not only for His own servants. He will not let any of us rest in our sins. Those who go against Him are not happy. He will not let them be—why?

So all the past twenty years He had been watching these men—they had the keen pain of an accusing conscience. They did not like to talk of it even to each other. But they would sometimes wake in the night and think of Joseph, and try to forget the memory of his face; and of the poor father's misery. Ah! conscience gives men a bad time if they will not give in. God put it there for that purpose. He never could get back sinners otherwise.

Do you think when the brothers got home, their consciences were easier? I don't think so. Tell me of their talk with their father. How often they must have wondered whether the silent old man had any suspicion of their cruelty to Joseph. He had kept his own counsel. But now, in his passion of grief, he lets it all out. He had suspected them all the time. How do you know? (*v.* 36). Surely, it must have touched them, too, to see his anxiety. And still more, when forced to let Benjamin go, to hear his earnest prayer as he bade him good-bye. Say it (xliii. 14). And every touching of their hearts was part of God's discipline for them.

§ 4. *The Dinner in Joseph's Palace*

Now they are back in Memphis, with the old dread and wonder upon them. But greater dread was to come. For scarce were they finished their purchases when

Joseph's steward nearly frightens them out of their wits. With what? Fancy an invitation to dinner! And in the governor's palace! They have already a fear of this masterful governor, with his mysterious power of calling up to them their sin. "What can this mean?" "What is he going to do to us?"

Now, can you make another picture in your minds? Joseph's dining-hall. Splendour and luxury, bright colours, strange, rude music, etc. The Egyptian guests (*v.* 32) are arriving. After them, the ten brothers, timid and embarrassed. The governor is there with his young wife, the Princess Asenath. She is watching with interest the ten country brothers, especially the handsome younger one, so like her husband. Then they bring the presents, and receive Joseph's courtly greeting: "Are you well? Is your father well, the old man? etc. Is this your younger brother, of whom you told me?" Don't you think he was acting the stranger well? Do you think it was easy? What blessing did he pronounce on Benjamin? Ah, that blessing nearly finished him. As he looked into the face of his only brother, the only other child of the beautiful young mother who had died that far-back day near Bethlehem, he felt something rise in his throat again, and he had to rush out of the hall. And when Asenath went to find him, what did she see? Yes, the great ruler of Egypt sobbing like a big child, and could not restrain himself. Ah! his heart was too soft for a stern tester of men. Do you think he could be cruel and spiteful to his brothers? Don't you see all the sternness must have been for their good?

What happened next? Washes off traces of tears,

and comes back calm and dignified again. Allots places to the guests. And again the terror of the supernatural is on the brothers as this terrible Egyptian points them to their places. Why? (*v.* 33). He puts Reuben in first seat, then Simeon, then Levi, etc., all exactly according to their birth. I wonder if Asenath smiled at their terror. And then he tries another clever test to see if they are jealous of Benjamin? (*v.* 34). But I think he soon put them at their ease (*v.* 34). Such kindly hearts as Joseph have always the knack of doing that.

§ 5. *The Severest Test of All*

But the most searching test of all had yet to come. After the dinner they started homewards, proud, surely, and flattered at the honour done to them. Benjamin is safe. Simeon is set free. How good this lord of Egypt had been! How delighted the old father would be!

All very pleasant—but in the midst of all they hear the clatter of hoofs, and in a few moments they are surrounded by Joseph's bodyguard, and the old steward is bending sternly from his chariot to hurl his angry charge in their teeth. What? Fancy! to be thieves. It was a horrible charge. They, the sons of the honourable old Jacob in Canaan, must feel the shame of it deeply. At first they don't believe it. What do they propose? Can't you picture their faces as sack after sack is emptied—seven, eight, nine, ten; surely it is a mistake! Ah, but just as the last sack is emptied, there is a groan of horror. They hear the clink of metal, and see the bright goblet as it rolls upon the sand!

So this petted Benjamin is a thief after all! He who is more valued in our father's eyes than the whole of us put together. He is a thief, and we are disgraced and ruined! This terrible Egyptian will make an end of us now.

Show me how this tested their attitude? Don't you see it? Why, if Joseph had given them a chance like that twenty years ago, don't you think their knives would have settled the question soon? Or, at any rate, they would have willingly left him to his fate. But marvellous is the change that is passing over their lives. They did not know it themselves. They did not know how they had got to love "the lad" till this great crisis forced them out of themselves. They will stick to him at any cost. Guilty or not guilty, he is their brother, and it would kill the dear old father if anything should happen to him. Besides, I think they feel that God is dealing with them. They feel it is all a just retribution; and, humbled and bowed down beneath His hand, "they rent their clothes, and laded every man his ass and returned to the city."

How does Joseph receive them? (xliv. 15). Do they resent it? No; they have no heart to resent it. They feel that One higher than Joseph has controversy with them. Utterly humbled, they can only say, "God hath found out the iniquity of thy servants." What do they propose? (*v.* 16). Does Joseph accept this? Do you see how his suggestion tests them still more? Unless they really loved the lad, they would accept that way out of their trouble, and neither Jacob nor anybody else could blame them much. What happens? (Teacher, read for class this exquisite speech of Judah—read it with care and feeling; it is one of the purest bits of true natural eloquence in the whole of literature.)

No wonder Joseph could not restrain himself; the sternness, which had been only assumed, vanished—

"I AM JOSEPH, YOUR BROTHER;"

and he fell upon Benjamin's neck and wept, and Benjamin wept upon his neck; and he kissed all his brethren, and wept upon them.

§ 6. *How the Divine Brother Deals with His Brethren*

What is the lesson of this story for us all? (Let the pupils guess, and then show the teaching as indicated here.) It is often said that Joseph is a type of our Lord. Perhaps he is; but with children I don't care to talk too much of men as "types." I want them to feel that Joseph is a real man, working out his real, actual life just as we do; not a figure set up to exhibit certain analogies.

We know that he was guided by God so to deal with his brethren as to produce in them what? Conviction of sin. It is, therefore, a picture of God's dealing with men—a picture of the great Divine Brother dealing with His brethren, if by any means He may produce in them conviction of sin. He cannot get them back otherwise. Why do people listen so carelessly to teaching of Christ's love, and atonement, and pardon for sin? Because they are not convicted of sin. If you could see—how often you have disappointed Him, and how lovingly He bears with you, you would be touched. So He has to deal with people as Joseph with his brothers; but alas, not always so successfully. He wants to make them sorry, and bring them back to Himself. So sometimes He lets them have a famine in their lives, i.e. they feel a want; they feel restless and worried, and dissatisfied, and in need of something; they hardly know what. Or sometimes sorrow and the loss of friends. Sometimes He has to take little child away from mother; or sometimes He sends trouble, and pain, and disgrace; something that reminds them and pains them about their sins. Are these pleasant? No, and often people get vexed with the Lord, and say, "Much He cares, indeed, if He lets such things happen." Does He care all the time? But still He lets the sore discipline go on, and ceases not at all for our crying and pain. And we are like Joseph's brothers. They thought Joseph hard. They could not see his anxiety, and yearning, and tears. When did they find out what Joseph really was? And so with us all. When people find out their sin and their neglect of Christ, and feel—"We are verily guilty concerning our Brother. We have sinned against Him, and neglected and disappointed Him. And now we are coming back to ask for His forgiveness"—then we find that He had been caring all the time; that He had been letting us have the pain and weariness only for our own good, that they might bring us to Himself.

QUESTIONS FOR LESSONS XX AND XXI

How did it happen that Joseph met his brothers again?

What was Joseph's Egyptian name and who was his wife?

Why do you think he did not at once reveal himself to his brothers?

How did he treat them?

Was not this cruel of him?

What was the result?

How did he surprise them at the dinner?

The ten brothers were now eleven?

What was his final test as to their feeling towards Benjamin?

This dealing with his brothers reminds us of our Lord—how?

LESSON XXII

JOSEPH AND HIS FATHER

Genesis XLV., XLVI. to v. 8, and v. 26 to end

§ 1. Joseph Declares Himself

Recapitulate last Lesson. Where did we stop? With telling that, after the passionate appeal of Judah, Joseph could no longer restrain himself. And so to-day we, as it were, raise the curtain on the same scene. The Egyptians have been asked to retire. The brothers are standing before him, frightened and excited. They have already noticed that queer breaking in his voice. It has greatly surprised them. But there is a greater surprise in store. For scarce has the heavy curtain fallen behind the departing Egyptians, when, to their utter bewilderment, this great governor of Egypt stretches forth his hand to them. What does he say? "I am Joseph!"

Were they delighted? (*v.* 3). Can't you imagine them starting back like frightened animals? "What does this terrible, mysterious Egyptian mean? He knew even our poor brother's name!" And then he repeats it again with an addition—what? (*v.* 4). Surely nobody but Joseph could know of that! They stare stupidly at him, utterly dumbfounded. And as they stare, slowly the face of the great Zapenath Paneah seems to change into the likeness of their lost brother. Surely, it must be Joseph after all! Do you think they are delighted now? Why not? Afraid of what? Yes, I should think they had, as the French say, a very "bad quarter of an hour." Should not you have, if in their place? And I think the most beautiful touch of the whole story is the exquisite delicacy with which he feels their position, and tries to comfort them. Tell me of it (*v.* 5). What a keen sympathy he had! What an unselfish, loving heart, that hated to see them troubled! "Don't fret—it was not you that sent me. It was God." Was that true? Then, were they not to blame for their wickedness? (Let the class try to puzzle out this difficulty for themselves. Try to interest them in it, and make it real for them; but don't explain it if they fail. The explanation comes better later on. Tell them they must leave this puzzle for a little while, and talk of Joseph's faith.)

§ 2. Joseph's Practical Faith

All through Joseph's story what did we find to have been the strength of his life? The simple, honest belief that God was always near, and that God had a high plan and purpose for his life. Was he right? We can see it now better than he could at the time, for we see the end of the story.

You remember how 200 years before, God had told Abraham that Israel should go down into Egypt, and remain there for 400 years (Acts vii. 6). And we have watched the curious way in which God's will was carried out. Joseph sold—taken to Egypt—put in prison wrongfully—interpreting dreams—made ruler of Egypt. Then we see how the famine forced the brothers to go down; and how all the after events carried out God's plan. But did all these people—the brothers, and Potiphar, and Pharaoh, and the rest—*intentionally* carry out God's plan? Did they even know of it? Ah! that is the wonderful thing. That people without their own knowledge, and even against their will, carry out God's plans. All that men could see at the time was the jealousy of brothers, and the foolish favouritism of a father, and the sins and lies and self-seeking of people in Egypt, and one true, faithful life, being lived for God. But you, who have the whole history before you, see God overruling it all for His purpose, and carrying out His design. You see His design getting steadily accomplished, that the children of Israel should sojourn in Egypt. So to-day God has great purposes for the world. Are all the people trying to carry them out? No. But even those who are thwarting are overruled by Him. So He lets the free wills of men have free play, and yet gets His great purposes accomplished. But, though He turns men's evil designs to work out good, yet He punishes them for the evil designs. Don't you see that that is quite the just and fair thing to do? And that is the answer to the puzzle we had just now. God looks at men's motives. If they intend to do a wicked thing, they are punished for it. And then God, the great, wise ruler, overrules that wicked thing, that it shall not spoil His plans, or even that it shall help them.

Something of this about God's dealings Joseph learned by the experience of his life. Does everyone learn it? Who do? Those who are trying to do God's will, and live for Him. That is a great help to understanding God. "The secret of the Lord is with them that fear Him." Those who live truly see truly. The pure in heart see God. Joseph saw bad people seeming to triumph, and himself, though trying to serve God, getting into trouble. Yet he learned by slow degrees that God was ordering his life, and that therefore things would somehow come right in the end.

§ 3. *What Joseph Learned about God's Help*

But he learned something else very beautiful about God's plan. (xlv. 7). Can't you guess? That, where God helps and blesses a man, He intends always through him to help and bless other men.

When God called and blessed Abraham, it was that Abraham should be a blessing to many. When He selected the family of Israel for blessing, it was that through them "all the families of the earth should be blessed." And so here with Joseph. Now, can you find that in verse 7? Some people think that God's love and care for them means that it is entirely for their own sake, in order that they themselves should be happy and holy. They thank God for His care, and kindness, and love, and all His help to their own souls and bodies; but all the time they are doing very little to bless other people's souls and bodies. They completely misunderstand God. And so their little souls shrivel up in them through their selfishness.

Not so Joseph. He knew that God cared and planned for careless people, too. He could have understood our Lord's teaching about the hundred sheep—what teaching? (Luke xv.) He knew that his brothers were not good; but he knew, too, that he would be just as bad if he were selfishly satisfied to get good things from God which should be for himself alone. He could not be satisfied with such a thought. No man whose life is growing like to his Lord's can ever be content to look on the sin and misery of his brethren around, and comfort himself with the thought that God is caring and planning for him, and not for them. I read once a beautiful Scotch story of a dear old Christian woman teaching her grandchild of God's love to him, in this imperfect way. "But, grannie," said he, "what about the little ignorant boys in the back lanes, that get hungry and cold, and sometimes fight and curse, and say bad words?" "My child, God only loves His own dear children. He cannot care for those who are not serving Him." The little boy looked at her, puzzled for a moment; then, with that strange, Christ-like instinct that is often in children, he horrified the dear old grannie by retorting: "If He don't care for them, grannie, I don't want Him to care for me!"

Ah, you see, Joseph had learnt God's love better than that dear old grannie. He knew God had a Divine plan for all, and that when they broke loose from it, He would make them miserable, in order to bring them back. Just what he himself had been doing with his brothers; and so he knew that when God helps and blesses His faithful children, it is that they may help and watch over the others.

§ 4. *The Message to His Father*

Next comes the beautiful message to his father. Read me *vv.* 9-13. Was not it a loving message? Was not it beautifully natural, too, that he should be so anxious to have his father proud of him? (*v.* 13). "Tell him of all my glory." If you went away, and became a great man, would you not delight that father and mother should see you, and be proud of their boy?

One thing always puzzles me—I wonder if it puzzles you—that Joseph never sought out his father all these years. But I feel pretty sure there was some reason which we don't know. First, he was a slave; then, a prisoner; perhaps something else hindered afterwards. From the moment he sees his brothers his heart goes out towards his father. Little they thought how eagerly he was asking, "Is your father well?" Little Judah thought how he was wringing his heart as he pictured the old father grieving at home, and told that he would die if evil came to Benjamin. And now see his eagerness—"Haste and bring down my father."

Do you think there was no disadvantage to him in bringing down his father and brothers? Read *ch.* xlvi., end of *v.* 34. Shepherds an abomination. We are told, too, by ancient writers how intensely proud the Egyptians were, and how sharp was their caste prejudice, and that shepherds and cattle-men were the most utterly despised and degraded—like scavengers or crossing-sweepers with us. Now, remember that Joseph was a great nobleman, and that the proud, jealous nobility of Egypt who were under him would think much less of him if his family of shepherds came to live with him. Do you think a meaner type of man would have been so quick to bring them? But Joseph was above all such littleness. I daresay he thought of it, but he would not let it influence him.

§ 5. *Three Pictures*

First Picture

Now shut your eyes and make these pictures in your mind. Old Jacob sitting in his big, black tent, with all the women and children around him, all listening to the wonderful story which the sons from Egypt were telling. Why, it was like a fairy-tale—all about kings, and nobles, and palaces, and beautiful cities; all about Joseph's splendid home, and the young Egyptian princess, his wife, and all the glory and power he had in Egypt.

The old man is completely overcome. He falls back fainting at the shock. When he recovers, he flatly refuses to believe a word of it. Then they lift him up, and get him his staff, and help him out into the sunshine, and show him the waggons, and chariots, and drivers, and the guard of honour—the costly presents from the mighty noble who was once his little boy in that very tent. And at last the spirit of the old man revived. "It is enough, it is enough. Joseph, my son, is yet alive. I will go and see him before I die!"

Second Picture

A great plain in Goshen, near where the famous battle of Tel-el-Kebir was fought by the English about forty years ago. The black tents of the Hebrew shepherds are pitched. Their flocks and herds are feeding on the plain; but no one is minding them. The splendid cavalcade of the Egyptian governor is approaching, and there is great excitement in Jacob's company. The children are watching the beautiful uniforms. The women are wondering what Asenath will be like.

But the poor old father's heart is filled with one great craving—"My boy is coming, my boy is coming. Let me see Joseph and die!" And now he knows that the first of the chariots has stopped; he hears his son's voice, that he has never forgotten; he feels the strong arms round his tottering frame. And as he looks with glad, proud, satisfied eyes at his little Joseph, now grown to be the great lord of Egypt, can't you imagine you hear that sigh of deep satisfaction—"Now let me die, since I have seen thy face, because thou art yet alive!"

Third Picture

They are sitting together in the tent. The old father, now grown very weak and grey, and the strong, stately governor of Egypt, with his jewelled collar and his splendid robes, sitting at his father's feet, as when he was a boy long ago. How very happy they are! How much they have to talk about! All that has happened in Canaan these twenty years—all the marvellous story of Joseph's adventures in Egypt; how he was sold in the slave market; how he was put into prison; how he got placed at the head of the whole land of Egypt. All about God's goodness to him; his happy home, and his young wife, and his two boys, and all his power. I think it was the gladdest day that ever came to Jacob and Joseph.

§ 6. Lesson

This is God's beautiful inspired picture to tell you what He loves to see between parents and children. Through their love for you God has given you a great power over the poor fathers and mothers. You have great power to hurt them or to gladden them. No one else on earth has that same power over them. He has, as it were, placed your hands upon their heart-strings, that by the slightest twist you can torture them as you will. Aye, and with the slightest touch you can gladden them, too.

I have seen fathers and mothers growing pale and sorrowful, heart-broken with sorrow that their children had given. And I have seen fathers and mothers proud and glad, like Jacob, because their children were a pride and a gladness to them. And I know that God, who has given that power to the children, is watching very carefully to see how they use it.

QUESTIONS FOR LESSON XXII

Tell of Joseph revealing himself to his brothers.

Did they enjoy it?

How did he try to set them at ease?

State pretty fully his message to his father?

There would be some unpleasantness in bringing down his family?

Can you make in words the three little pictures of Joseph meeting his father?

LESSON XXIII

AT JACOB'S DEATH-BED

Genesis XLVIII. v. 15 to end, and XLIX. to v. 27

Remember last Lesson. Waggons going down to Canaan for Jacob; the eager delight of the old man at the thought of meeting Joseph—that beautiful, touching scene, when the great ruler of Egypt in his state robes sat in the old black tent beside his father, as in the old days of his childhood, and told him all the story of his life. (Teacher must take trouble to prepare this recapitulation so as to touch the feelings of the children; otherwise he loses much of the interest of the present Lesson.)

§ 1. Beside a Father's Death-Bed

Now we go on with the story. Seventeen years (*ch.* xlvii. 28) have elapsed since the meeting in the old black tent. Joseph is in the prime of his life, rejoicing in his splendid work for Egypt. His two boys are grown up; done school; probably at college in their mother's city of On, the Oxford or Harvard of ancient Egypt, where it is said Moses was educated long afterwards—"in all the wisdom of the Egyptians." But, as they are growing

217

stronger, do you think the old grandfather in Goshen is growing stronger too?

So, one day, there comes to Joseph the hurried message. What? (xlviii. 1). What does he do? Who go with him? Do you think Jacob was glad? (*v.* 2). Why, he nearly got well with the pleasure of it! And then Joseph sits down beside him in the dark tent, and the old man talks to him, as old men love to talk, about the old, far-back days. Yes; about his long life, and the goodness of God, and the promises to his race; and one other memory of a deep pain which neither of them could ever forget. What? (*v.* 7). Ah! poor old man, nobody but Joseph could ever fully enter into that trouble with him. Don't you think it was nice to talk it all over with Joseph? Don't you think it was nice for Joseph, too? Ah! it is good to have these close relations between father and son remaining unbroken as the years go by. God's blessing always goes with them. Sometimes sons and daughters miss this. As they grow up, and new interests come, the old interests die out, and they forget about the dear old father and mother whose hearts are bound up in them. What does God say of it in Fifth Commandment? Be quite sure of this, that no blessing from God can come to any of us who forget or neglect the old father or mother.

§ 2. Ephraim and Manasseh

There is one part of the conversation which we have passed over. It is a plan which Jacob had to propose about Joseph's two sons. What? (*vv.* 5, 6). Yes, they were to take their place as members of the family of Israel.

Do you think most fathers in Joseph's position would have cared for this? Remember Jacob and his sons in Egypt were despised shepherds, people looked down on as "abominations to the Egyptians." Remember that Joseph was higher than the greatest nobles of the land; that his sons would be like young nobles in position; that the best posts in Egypt would probably be open to them if they cared to give up their connection with Israel. When a man has won such a grand position as Joseph had, it would be quite natural that he should wish to hand it on to his children. Did Joseph consent to his father's proposal? Yes. He knew that God was especially with Israel, and had a great purpose in the future of blessing it, and blessing the world through means of it, and it seemed to him that God's blessing and a share in God's purpose were of more value than all the wealth and honour that Egypt could give. Don't you think that the young nobles of Egypt would think Ephraim and Manasseh very silly? Do *you* think so? It is good to have wealth and high position if it be with God's blessing. But it is better to remain poor and unnoticed all our days rather than miss the best thing that God has to give, i.e., His blessing on our lives and a share in His great purpose of helping the world.

But in the midst of all the talking and planning, Jacob and Joseph seem to have almost forgotten the presence of the two boys. I should think they would be getting rather impatient by this time. I expect they made some noise which drew Jacob's attention. Why did he not see them before? (*v.* 10). Was he pleased? Did he think of God in his pleasure? (*v.* 11). Men who know God best, feel that all their good things come from Him. He told Joseph to bring them to Him. What for? What surprised Joseph in the blessing? I think it is beautiful to have religion so real in a home that the old grandfather's first thought on meeting his grandsons is to bless them in God's name. I don't think the boys would ever forget that day when they knelt beside their grandfather's death-bed, and heard that wonderful prayer. Say it for me (*vv.* 15, 16). It is only in religious homes such things can occur.

§ 3. Blessing the Twelve Tribes

After blessing Joseph and his boys, the old man was growing steadily weaker. He felt death drawing very near. So he directs that all his sons should be sent for, that they might hear his last words.

Very solemn thing at any time is a gathering of sons around a father's death-bed. But this was a much more important matter than an ordinary gathering at a death-bed. It was, in a sense, the formal founding of the Israelite nation, and sending it forth for God's great purpose. What purpose? That they should keep alive the knowledge of God in the world, and that, finally, through them the Messiah should come, in whom all the families of the earth should be blessed. So, I think, God gave Jacob the spirit of prophecy to tell in outline the future of his race, and to give some hints even of Messiah, the King who should reign in peace.

When a wise, religious old man like Jacob is near death, he can see things with more clearness than others, and have clearer ideas of what is likely to come. He knew well the characters of these sons. After fifty years watching them, he ought to know them, and be able to guess what they would probably do. But this would not account for the fact that his prophecies about their tribes through many centuries came in a great measure true, or for the fact that after deposing Reuben from the chief place he should be guided to put Judah in it instead; not Joseph, his favourite, whom we should have expected. And especially would it not account for that strange, far-off thought in his mind of some great Being whom he calls SHILOH—or Prince of Peace—who should come out of Judah, and to whom "should the gathering (or obedience) of the people be."

I think there was much *common sense* in the old man's judgment of character, and marvellous *faith* in his actually allotting and dividing a land of which he did not yet own a single foot, except a grave; but there is more than common sense, and more than faith. The wisest students of Scripture have agreed in believing that it was under the guidance of God's Spirit that he was able to see, not clearly perhaps, but in some dim, indistinct manner, a vision of the accomplishing of God's purpose for Israel.

The whole speech is in the Hebrew a long poem. Perhaps it was afterwards made into poetry, to be more easily remembered; or perhaps the exalted spiritual excitement of the dying man uttered it in such form. We do not know. Now tell me his opinion of first three sons. Good or bad? Does the badness affect their future, and that of their descendants? Reuben is deposed from the privilege of the firstborn, and of Simeon and Levi we read —what? (end of *v.* 7). And all this came true. Reuben never did excel—no judge, or ruler, or prophet came from his tribe. In Numbers ii. 9, 10, we see Judah take first place, and Reuben go in second rank. And so high did Judah rise in after days, that the whole nation became known by his name. We see Simeon weakest of all the tribes (Numbers xxvi. 14). In Moses's blessing, Simeon is omitted entirely. In distribution of the land, it was merely scattered among the tribe of Judah, having only certain parts assigned within the inheritance of Judah (Joshua xix. 1-9). And the Levites had no inheritance, but were scattered in separate cities all over the tribes. But these Levites must have grown to be better men than their ancestors. Why? You know they were chosen to be the clergy of Israel.

All this has a lesson for us. What? That men make their own future. That the future of each is influenced by his past. Reuben, and Simeon, and Levi probably did not think that their wrong-doing would affect themselves and their descendants for centuries to come. But it did. So people sometimes think about heaven; that after a careless, wasted life here, they can somehow fly off, like the swallows, to an eternal summer after their death. Can they? No. The future is always made by the past. But there is a lesson of hope in Levi's history. What? That no man's future need necessarily be a curse, even if he have spoiled the past. True sorrow and change of purpose will be received by God, and good and blessing will come in the future to a wrong-doer who repents, though not all that might have been if he had not done wrong.

§ 4. Shiloh

Who is the next son? Yes; and his blessing is the most important of all. Joseph's blessing we have already discussed, and the other tribes are not so important to learn. So, we give remainder of time to Judah's blessing.

How does Judah come out in the history of Joseph? Twice we read of him, and both times good. What? But that is not what makes his blessing so important. What does? (*v.* 10). Who, do you think, is meant by Shiloh? Our Lord? Yes. All our best commentators give that explanation.

The Jewish Targums or paraphrases of Genesis add the name "Messiah" here. All the more ancient Jews hold it to be a prophecy of Messiah. The word "Shiloh" would mean "peaceable," or "peace-giver," or "peace;" and evidently Jacob looks forward to the coming of Shiloh as something very great and desirable. But some have doubted as to whether Jacob really meant Christ, or had any clear thought or knowledge of Him. Probably he had only very dim views, and only saw that some great Peace-giver should come in the far future for the accomplishment of God's purpose. But perhaps, on the other hand, God revealed to him more than we think. You know our Lord said that Abraham rejoiced to see His day (St. John viii. 5, 6). I don't know how much that means. Perhaps Jacob saw His day, too, as death came near. I have read a curious suggestion as to where Jacob learned this beautiful name. The commentator reminds us that at Peniel Jacob asked the mysterious angel His name. The angel replied: "Wherefore dost thou ask after my name?" And He blessed him there. "I have sometimes thought," adds this writer, "that as He blessed him, He whispered in his ear this lovely title, and that it lingered in the old man's mind through all these years."

All we can definitely say about the matter is, that most of our best commentators look on this as a prophecy of our Lord, to whom "shall the gathering [or the obedience] of the people be." It does not really matter if we cannot be quite sure as to how much Jacob meant. We have prophecies enough of which there is no doubt. For, from this time forward all through the Psalms and Prophets we see the growing hope of some great coming One. We shall learn about these later on when we come to the Life of our Lord.

QUESTIONS FOR LESSON XXIII

Tell of Jacob's death.

Tell his plan and his blessing for his two grandsons.

Tell his prophecy of "Shiloh." What did it mean?

Repeat his blessing on Joseph.

Meaning of "a fruitful bough by a well"?

Why had the Levites no inheritance?

THE DEATH OF JOSEPH

Genesis XLIX. 27 to end, and L.

Remember last Lesson. Remind briefly of Jacob's death-bed, and the blessing of his sons. After this he must have been utterly exhausted. But he had one direction to give before he died. What? Why would he not be content to be buried in Egypt? Was it merely to be laid in the grave with his kindred? What else? (*ch.* xlviii. 21). He knew that some day God would lead the Israelites back to the Promised Land, and he did not want his bones to lie in a strange land.

And now comes the close of old Jacob's story. How is his death described? (*ch.* xlix. 33). Now, at the close of his life, do you think God's warning and discipline had done him good? Do you think he was a better man than on that day when he cheated Esau out of his birthright? Poor old man, God had led him through a hard path—but it was a very blessed path, since it made him a noble and holy man. So we bid good-bye to Jacob. How do you think they all felt at his death? All very sorry, I daresay. But one above all was? How did poor Joseph take it? (*ch.* l. 1). Many a man has cried like that since. But Joseph had not the bitter self-reproach that comes to many a man when he stands by his dead father. That day will come to most of us. Remember that on that day there will be untold pain at the remembrance of every neglect; then will be the purest, truest pleasure in the memory of every word of his approval and gratitude. It will be like the ringing of joy-bells in your heart for ever, if he should say to you then, "My son, I thank God for the comfort you have been to me all the days of my life."

§ 1. *Misunderstood*

Then they had a magnificent funeral in Canaan. Tell me something about this grand funeral? Why all the honour done to Jacob by the Egyptians?

Then Joseph came home after the funeral to his wife and his boys, and scarce was he well settled at home when a very disappointing surprise came to him. Tell me about it? (*vv.* 15-18). Why should it be a disappointment? Poor Joseph! with all his love, and his suppressed feelings, and his longing to forgive. He thought they believed in him. And now to find that all the time they had been mistrusting him, and thinking it was only their father's presence that saved them. Ungenerous souls never can understand a free, generous forgiveness. It was enough to disgust him, and utterly embitter him. Did it? What did he say? (*vv.* 19-21). Nothing could embitter a man who lived so close to God. I reminded you lately of his father's opinion of him. What? (*ch.* xlix. 22, 23). "A fruitful bough *by a well*," i.e., with his roots running down into the cool, fresh springs; therefore did his branches run over the wall. "The archers sorely grieved him, and shot at him." Aye did they! Ill-treated him, and wronged him, and told lies of him. Did that embitter him, and sour his life? Why not? (xlix. 24). Ah, that is it. Men living for God, like Joseph, never let these things harm them, or make them bitter.

Have any of you ever felt vexed at being misunderstood, or having lies told about you? Did it make you feel cross and bitter? That is the worst harm these things can do. Make you bitter, shut up your hearts, sour your affections. If you don't let them do that you rob them of their power. Men like Joseph never let them do that. They simply turn back to God, and tell Him of the vexation. They say, "Lord, *you* don't misunderstand me; you don't believe the false charge against me—and that is what I care most for." This helps them to make allowance for the person who has thus hurt them, and who perhaps really had some excuse for his action— perhaps had been told lies by another about them, and believed them. So they say, "Lord, perhaps this man did not mean to hurt me, or perhaps he thought I was wrong. In any case I can't afford to get soured and spoiled, for then I should be less lovable, and less able to serve Thee."

§ 2. A Good Old Age

Little more is told of the story of Joseph. He grew

to a good old age. How old? Until the grandsons of his two boys were climbing on his knees (*v.* 23). I think that means that he was fond of them.

Some old people delight to have children about them. I am sure Joseph was a dear, lovable old man. I think of him with the little boys on his knee, telling them stories of his boyhood in Haran; of his being sold as a slave; or the old story, that his own father used to tell him in his childhood, of the beautiful angels that appeared to him on the giant stairs at Bethel. I do like to see old people fond of children. I am sure Joseph's sons and grandsons liked to be near him. It should always be so with old people. It *will* always be so if they are living sweet unselfish lives for God, *and if the boys and girls are doing the same.* Sometimes children are a perfect nuisance, when they are spoiled, and selfish, and disagreeable. It is very sad for old people to have to live in such a home. It is the sweet, unselfish Christ-like lives that make the homes and the old people happy always.

And so at last Joseph died. How much of Exodus is taken up with his death? One line. How much with his life? Count the chapters. Fourteen chapters about his life, and only one line about his death. Why? Because a man's death is not the important thing, but his life. Some people now think far more of what sort of death-bed a man has, and whether he had much feeling of hope and love towards God, when he was dying, more than they think of the whole tenor of his life before. It is very pleasant when dying people have such feelings; but it is not the test of their state. Some careless people can talk piously on death-beds, and some of the most faithful lives have passed away in heavy stupor or distress of mind. You remember the great trouble of our Lord's mind near the very end. Therefore, in most cases pious death-bed sayings are only of value if they are in keeping with the life. And servants of Christ, who die unconscious or troubled, are just as safe in His everlasting arms as if they had had the most joyful death-beds. It is the purpose of the life that matters. The death does not matter much; therefore the Bible does not deal much with death-beds.

§ 3. *"By Faith, Joseph——"*

One death-bed saying of Joseph has come down to us. What? (*vv.* 24, 25). Strong and deep as ever on his death-bed was, you see, that faith in the living God which had kept him all his life. Sometimes I fancy he needed it then more than people generally think. Perhaps the shadow of the coming hard times was on him and his people already.

It was now how many years since he first stood before Pharaoh? (*ch.* xli. 46 and l. 26). In eighty years many things happen. Pharaoh probably dead. Perhaps Joseph's great services forgotten. Nations are often ungrateful enough to their benefactors. I don't know. But it seems to me that the ending of the story is sad. I notice that the old man talks of the hope that "God will visit you," as if there was already some shadow of coming trouble. And I notice that he is not buried in Canaan at once, like his father, and that there is no word of a splendid funeral like Jacob's. Perhaps the time of Joseph's glory was over. I don't know. But, if it were so, I know it would not matter too much to him. He had lived very close to God, in a region where earthly honours do not make too deep an impression; and in his death he shows where his heart has been all the time of his grandeur. What did he make them promise? "When God visits you, and fulfils His ancient promise, swear unto me that ye will carry up my bones." And the whole clan swore unto him that they would.

Then we are told he died, and they embalmed him, and put him in a coffin, or a mummy case, in Egypt. Ever see a mummy case in museum? We can see the mummy now of the Pharaoh who oppressed Israel, and we can buy his photograph for a few pence. I wonder if we shall ever find Joseph's? Perhaps some of the Egyptian mummies that we have touched in museums were of people whom Joseph knew. Would it not be interesting to see Joseph, and touch him? A very wonderful influence had that dead body of Joseph in his mummy case. For hundreds of years it lay in some secret cave in Egypt. Many kings arose, and died, and were buried, and still the Israelites remained in Egypt, and still the oath of Joseph lay on them, and still the secret of the mummy's cave was handed down through all the centuries of slavery, till nearly 500 years afterwards, when the Israelites were set free. On that awful night, with the Egyptians wailing over the dead first-born, and the Israelites hurried and excited at their departure, they did not forget Joseph. They opened the cave, and Moses took the bones of Joseph, etc. (Exodus xiii. 19).

Curious to think of that dead Joseph in his mummy case, and the influence he exercised all that time? When they were comfortable, and inclined to settle down in Goshen, their promise to Joseph was always reminding them that God had a higher purpose for them somewhere in the future. And when they were under the lash of the slave-drivers on any day of special misery, I fancy some of them would creep off to the dead man in the cave, and take comfort from the contagion of his mighty faith. They would say: "Joseph believed that God would deliver us, and give us the land promised to our fathers. Surely, it will be so; let us trust God; let us bear up a little longer." And so you see Joseph's faith in God, which had been such a power in all his own life, remained after his death a power to help the nation for hundreds of years.

§ 4. How God Buries His Workers, But Carries On His Work

Remember again God's promise to Abraham 300 years before, and His purpose of separating one nation for the good of all men, that through them religion should be preserved to the world. God said they should be in slavery for hundreds of years, and afterwards come back to accomplish the purpose of their calling.

Did Abraham see the promise fulfilled? Did Isaac? Did Jacob? What is said in Epistle to Hebrews? (xi. 13). No; "All these died in faith, not having received the promises, but," etc. And now Joseph dies, with less apparent likelihood of fulfilment than ever. He was probably the only one of his race in Egypt that cared much about them; and the end of him was to die, and be embalmed as a mummy. That is the last word of Genesis, and for centuries afterwards careless people in Europe or Goshen might smile at the foolishness of his faith.

But 500 years later comes Exodus, and then Joshua, and the Kings and Prophets, and at last the coming of Christ, and the long history of the Church. Does it look as if God had failed in His promise? God buries His workers. He can do without Abraham, or Jacob, or Joseph. No death stops God's plan. We, too, have to do our little work, to live, like Joseph, a pure, strong, brave, unselfish life; to do our little part to pull the poor old world straight; and then, like Joseph, in faith and peace, leave ourselves and the great future of the world to Him.

QUESTIONS FOR LESSON XXIV

Disappointing questions that came to Joseph after his father's funeral?

How did he take it?

How many years between Joseph's first appearance before Pharaoh and Joseph's death?

Why do we think that he loved children?

How much space is given to story of his life and how much to the story of his death? Why?

What vow did he demand as he died?

Show from history that God's will got accomplished in spite of all obstacles.